Letters from the Dales

THE DIPPER

LETTERS FROM THE DALES

W R MITCHELL

CASTLEBERG
1994

For
Perry Austin-Clarke
Editor of the *Telegraph & Argus*
(in whose pages much of the material
in this book first appeared).

A **Castleberg** Book.

First published in the United Kingdom in 1994.

Copyright © W R Mitchell 1994.

The moral right of the author has been asserted.

ISBN 1 871064 99 6

Typeset in Palacio, printed and bound in the United Kingdom by
Lamberts Printers, Station Road, Settle, North Yorkshire, BD24 9AA.

Published by Castleberg, 18 Yealand Avenue, Giggleswick, Settle,
North Yorkshire, BD24 0AY.

Contents

Illustrations...

Acknowledgements to the Dalesman Publishing Company.
Title page, also pages 27 and 44, Richard Bancroft.
Pages 18 and 21, Ionicus.

Introduction

THIS DALES anthology is light-hearted, folksy and anecdotal. Almost fifty years have elapsed since my travels for *The Dalesman* magazine began with a trip on the morning bus into Littondale. I intended to walk back but it began to rain, as it sometimes does in the Dales. The driver of a small lorry said: "Thou can either get on t'back, in t'cab or on t'running board." In the back was steaming manure; the cab held three men and a dog; so I stood on the running board—all the way back to Grassington.

In those days, the Dales belonged to Dalesfolk and had that delicate quality we call charm. Mostly, it was so quiet you could hear the wax crackling in your ears. At night, if the village lantern (the moon) was not shining, it was truly dark. There was no general orange glow, as there is today from sodium chloride lighting which is reflected back from the clouds.

Half a century ago, when I became a freeman of the Dales through my connection with *The Dalesman,* almost all the farms were occupied and families were large. Hired men were common. At farms on the marginal lands, they still milked the few cows by hand, the jets of milk spurting against the side of a pail.

Apart from village shops and services the roads leading to Dales villages held travelling shops of various kinds. Mr Hugill, who arrived from Burnley with a van full of hardware, was a descendant of a Swaledale lead-miner who, when the industry slumped, moved his family to East Lancashire, where there would be work for the lasses in t'mills.

Dales life has been transformed by tractors and machines. I had seven years of voluntary haytiming on Handby

Ewbank's farm at Austwick. In the first year, the work of Handby's lile grey Ferguson was augmented by Frank Lambert's hoss, Peggy, which passed wind at every footfall. Next year, Peggy was absent. She had been sold for meat! So much for Dales sentiment.

Now mechanised up to the hilt, the Dales farmer can manage with a little seasonal help, plus his wellies and a bundle of binder twine, used to hold up his trousers and fettle up everything from gates to machines. A Dentdale farmer had an ill-matching pair of wellingtons, one being black and one green. I suggested it was unusual. "Nay," he replied, "my son's getten a pair just like 'em."

The colour scheme of the Dales is not as it was, following a top-of-the-dale switch from grassland to conifer forest and from dual-purpose Shorthorns, whose milk was made into butter or cheese, to beef stock with unspellable Continental names. The marginal land is littered with the shells of little farmsteads, each of which offered a living of a sort to a large family.

A Swaledale friend tells me that, since he was a lad, one hundred and twenty smallholdings between Reeth and Keld have lost their separate identity. He shakes his head at once lonely moors which have been shredded to provide tracks for vehicles so that grouse-shooters do not have to walk.

The Dales villages are tidier than they were, with evidence of the urban mind in the hanging baskets and flower-bedecked wheelbarrows on trim lawns. Barns have been splendidly transformed into houses. Modern outbuildings look like aircraft hangers. At a farm on the hills near Malham, where new buildings have gone up at the speed of mushrooms, the farmer said to his sons: "I reckon 'at if somebody built a pub, this'd be a village."

Many field barns have been ransacked for their stone and slate. One of my favourite barns, near Stackhouse, disappeared while I was on holiday. Now you can scarcely tell where it stood. The Dales' celebrated flower-fields are restricted to a few grant-aided tracts of land. With more cattle and sheep on the better land—"thou hes to run to stand still these days, lad"—the herby grass was turned "brown side up" by the plough and now there's a wall-to-wall carpet of ryegrass so that there's the same shade of green throughout. Haytime has gone; the grass is ensiled, stuffed in to black plastic bags and laid out at the edges of meadows like so many black slugs.

The Dales retain their appeal for me. I can still thrill to the sight of U-shaped valleys, V-shaped gills, bare sheep ridges, forming low horizons under a big sky. The Dales have bluebell woods, waterfalls crying out like prophets in the wilderness, circling curlews and, of course, those in- domitable farmers, fighting the ancient battle against the weather, long winters and thin soils.

They are still busy. My father-in-law told of going to Hawes auction with a farmer friend who, when they were not being promptly attended at a local cafe, brought his stick down on the table and said: "Come on, missus, we're not on us holidays!" The farmer's son moves at high speed on his all- terrain vehicle, with a light-alloy crook beside him and a dog riding pillion.

I have briefly touched on Dales weather. Don't expect too much from it. That big sky often has clouds which are mucky. But when the sun does shine—when cumulus clouds drift like wool-sacks across an azure sky—there's no lovelier region on earth.

The Dalesfolk have always been a race apart, evolving in isolation, with a strong Norse heritage of pastoral farming and the Norse aversion to crowds. An exception was on market day, such as in my native town of Skipton, where (in my youth) you would always recognise a farmer because he had tweedy clothes, a cap with a neb to it, breeches and brown leggings and boots so well polished they winked back at the sun.

Men and women segregated as soon as their cars—springy

cars with clattering engines—came to a halt, the men making a bee-line for t'auction mart and the women making slow progress up the High Street, gossiping with neighbours they only saw in Skipton, patronising old-established grocery firms like Stockdale and Helm and having tea and cream cake (a wicked extravagance) at Whitakers or the Castle Cafe.

I entered the mart with a sense of adventure in case a bullock ran free or I was in danger of being overwhelmed by a group of sheep which had broken away from a drover and now had to run the gauntlet of men with sticks. The farmer who appeared to lunge at a sheep was deliberately sinking his hands through wool to its back and, in an instant, assessing its merits or de-merits. It is said that a motorist, who was weary of trailing sheep being driven to the mart—the animals were milling about, rather than moving in an orderly fashion—asked a perspiring drover: "Who is the master of this flock?" He replied: "Yon black-faced little begger at t'front."

I called this anthology Letters from the Dales because I wanted to develop an informal approach to Dales topics: the informality of the hastily-written letter. Like the Dalesfolk— each person a "character", with individual thought and action—this book must not become predictable or stilted. Hopefully, I have introduced a few novel thoughts and topics.

Winter Into Spring

The prevailing water-filled "westerlies" from the Atlantic bring a humid climate to the Pennine fells. This encourages the greenness which visitors admire and farmers welcome as an essential for the land on which their stock is reared.

Harry J Scott (1975).

The dales countryside has trout streams, grouse moors, sheep and cattle farming. Edible wild plants may be less common here in a landscape of stone walls than in parts of the country where hedgerows survive. None the less, there is luxuriant growth in places protected from the voracious appetites of sheep.

Janet Rawlins, A Dales Countryside Cookbook (1993).

We are sitting now in a farmhouse kitchen whose window looks on to the road. Conversation stops as we hear footsteps or a car approaching. We gaze out to see who it is. If there is any doubt, we settle between ourselves who it is likely to be.

Ella Pontefract, The Dalesman (1939).

The Curlews Return

A FARMER living high up Wharfedale said: "I reckon t'back o' winter's brokken when I hears t'curlew call."

Spring has been a little late this year. Long after the curlews returned to their nesting grounds, the high fells bore a crust of fresh snow. G K Yeates, the naturalist-photographer who lived in curlew country near Harrogate before moving South, wrote: "A curlew is not daunted by mere inclement weather."

In the off-season, I visit the edge of Morecambe Bay to listen to the drawl of curlews which are wintering by the sea. Where do our Dales birds go? Bill Shuttleworth, farmer-naturalist, who under licence attached light alloy rings to the legs of young curlews so that their future movements might be traced, told me of a "recovery" from wintering grounds by the Shannon in western Ireland. A south-westerly line of migration is indicated.

The first curlew I saw this year was cruising over the multi-laned Aire Valley road just north of Keighley. The bird descended towards a golf course. Subsequently, in North Ribblesdale, curlews—unseen but uttering contact calls—came in with the misty weather which presaged a thaw.

Birds are now widely spread but not as numerously as they were. Drainage and re-seeding of the valley land robbed birds of nesting cover and food. The marshy spots (known to some people as "tewit ground") are under grass. Now that silage-making is the rule, the first cut of grass comes at a vulnerable time for curlews—when the young are half-grown.

On a recent pilgrimage to upper Swaledale, I heard a springtime medley of bird calls, which infused new life into upland areas which during the winter heard only the guttural voices of red grouse or the honk of the carrion crow.

I crossed from Wensleydale via Buttertubs Pass and stopped near the limestone shafts so that I might listen for the Pennine nightingale—more properly known as ring-ouzel, the white-bibbed mountain blackbird, which is generally encountered at an elevation of over 1,000 ft. A cock bird's clear, cool notes resounded in the echo-chamber of a gill.

Over the marginal land, lapwings were giving exuberant "oo-ips" at the start of acrobatic displays which would have brought a whistle of astonishment from a member of the RAF display team. A buzzing sound from the tufty wings of a diving tewit warned me I was getting too near its nest.

A curlew rose steeply, hung in the air like a feathered kite and began its shallow song-glide on stiffened wings. The bird's aria started with low, drawn-out notes which developed into the well-known bubbling trill. More low notes gave the song a satisfactory conclusion.

The curlew has brought a response from North Country writers. John Hillaby, speaking at his moor-edge home in North East Yorkshire, described the curlew as "the symbol of the moors". Richard Kearton, who was born in upper Swaledale in 1862 and became a pioneer of nature photography, had a highly-emotional response to curlew calls: "I never hear a bird's thrilling notes without having my soul stirring to ecstacies within me."

The Dales had a curlew-busy sky. When 25 years ago, I researched for a book I called *A Year with the Curlews,* there seemed to be a nesting pair in every other field. One clutch of four pear-shaped eggs was laid in a shallow depression on a grass verse of the high road between Settle and Airton. At summer's end, a huge moulting flock of curlews assembled on the damp floor of the dale between Settle and Long Preston.

A pair of curlews is nesting about a quarter of a mile from my home. I hear the birds calling by night as well as day. Do these Dales curlews suffer from insomnia? Or is there a fox on the prowl?

Those Cute Stone Fences

IT'S AN eerie experience to be walking in the Dales during the calm of early morning when, suddenly, a dozen yards of drystone wall—weakened by the freeze-thaw of many winters—collapses with a clatter and cloud of dust. I leapt with surprise at the unexpected sound. So did a Dales sheep, one of a breed which nowadays does not bat an eyelid as a jet aircraft passes at zero-feet with a noise like a thunderclap.

An American who toured the Dales was full of enthusiasm for our mortarless walls, which she called "those cute stone fences". Sadly, many stretches of wall are crumbling. Farmers carry out only essential repairs. There is no time nor money to maintain the lesser walls.

The futuristic pattern of walls and a host of little field barns are features which help to make the Dales landscape unique in a European context. A Pennine wall is really two walls in one, tapering with height, bound together by rows of large stones called "throughs" and with some well-matched capstones to "turn" the weather.

If a wall is gapped, the material for its repair is on the spot. A waller like Geoff Lund, of Upper Wharfedale, works mainly by t'rack of t'eye in assessing which stone will fill a gap. He expertly appraises, without a geometric instrument, the progress of the "batter", which is the narrowing from bottom to top. When Yorkshire Television filmed Geoff's skill, his restless fingers removed a few courses from a wall and re-built it several times before the film crew were ready to record the process.

There is no deadening uniformity about the walls. In a good gritstone area, walling is almost as easy as using red

15

brick, whereas well-washed stone originally "out o' t'beck", needs a bit of sandpapering to make it stick. Or so I was told by a waller noted for his droll humour. A farmer tipped him a heap of beck-bottom stones for a walling job. When the farmer returned, several hours later, the heap had gone. He thought the stones had been used in the wall, but each had been rejected, tossed back in to the beck. The waller simply remarked: "I've drooned t'lot."

The walls faithfully reflect the geology of the Dales. No waller carried a stone further than was necessary. So the tone of the walls varies with the underlying geology. Limestone takes on various hues when wet, especially as the sun sets redly after a stormy day. Gritstone comes in various browns and Horton Flags, which outcrop in North Ribblesdale, are grey-blue.

Arthur Raistrick, the Dales historian, who lived at Linton-in-Craven, wrote that the true born north-country man would feel that something vital had been taken from the landscape if the walls were missing.

He distinguished between three main types of walls—first the maze of small enclosures near a village. These crooked eccentric walls were among the first to be built. Then there's the grid-iron pattern of the valley bottom and the lower slopes and, finally, the bee-line walls of the higher ground which parcel the moors into long strips.

The first type is well represented east of the beck between Malham and the Cove. Here are some of the oldest known walls. More recent stretches are said to "stand on one leg", having been built on a bank beside a lynchet (old ploughing strip). John Geldard, who farmed in this area for many years, told me that one noticeable change during his farming career was the disappearance of an entire wall, tossed in the beck— stone by stone, year after year—by high-spirited visitors.

The grid-iron pattern of walls are those of the Enclosure period, towards the end of the eighteenth century. Arthur Raistrick called the Great Enclosure "a tragedy for the small man", who lost his right of pasturage on the common, lost his bit of land and was compelled to become a wage labourer in a time of falling wages and rising cost of living. It was, nonetheless, the golden age of walling.

Walling is an individualistic job; it's not like an assembly kit, with a list of instructions to follow. It was the hallmark of a good waller that when he picked up a stone he could always "ken a place for it". In the Bolton Abbey district, "it were not so bad if you got some decent stone. If you got an area where you were bothered wi' a lot o' lile bits o' stone, you put a heck of a lot of stones on to t'wall and didn't git ower far."

In North Ribblesdale, where limestone was commonplace, wet stone was slippery and those who worked at the quarries, but also did a lile bit o' walling when necessary, used the leather "uppers" from old boots to protect their hands. A man cut holes in the leather through which he could put his thumb and forefinger.

A Dales wall is not a rigid structure. It shifts and settles. Norman Nicholson, the Cumbrian poet, claimed that a drystone wall actually walks. In a reading given in Horton-in-Ribblesdale Church one summer evening, he referred to a wall's constant subtle movement in a poem which describes the wall as a "grey millipede on slow stone hooves."

A good wall lasts over a century, if the foundations are good and joints are crossed. The old-time waller said: "End in and end out—one upon two and two upon one." A Yorkshire rood, used to assess payment, is seven yards. A good waller is beyond price. It was said of a man at Malham that he'd set off for a day's walling—and it took him two days to walk home again!

Dales dancers are a tough breed. An old couple related,
quite calmly, how they had driven to and from Dent on
a snowy road which had shrunk to the width of the
council's plough. For the men, the dance began with
arm-raising exercises at the local inn. One rough
wooden floor was made slippery by scattering a packet
of Lux all over it, and during the first few dances, no one
could hear the band for sneezing! The most dangerous
floor, an old Army hut in Coverdale, sloped towards a
cherry-red stove. Harry Cockerill, farmer and popular
accordianist, recalled: "Many a dance didn't begin till
midnight; the dancers nivver knocked off before two or
three o'clock. I used to "fodder" cows at outbarns on
my way home. Sometimes, when I got home, I was that
weary I didn't know if moon was going to bed or sun
was getting up!"

T'Owd-fashioned Sort o' Dancing

LOCAL "hops" have survived into a pop-mad world. They offer non-stop variety. The dancers use up as much energy as if they had been on a 20-mile walk.

Tosside, perched on a hilltop at an elevation of 800 ft., is a celebrated "dancing spot". Jackets are soon doffed and ties loosened as dancers "get a sweat on". Years ago, the last job at Tosside before dancing began was to remove the central coke stove. Two men advanced on it with iron barns—and carried it into the yard, where it thawed any lying snow.

Old-tyme dancing (to use a popular description of this vigorous form of recreation) seems to be a way to keep the ageing process at bay for people—mainly oldish people—who do not like sitting about. "There's nivver owt good on t'telly."

Meeting Peter Beresford in Settle the other day, we were soon chatting about Dales dancing. His family has been connected with it since the days when nearly every hamlet had its dances. In one tiny building, near the head of Wharfedale, the band had to sit on the billiards table. Sometimes, a dancer arrived back home just in time to change into working togs and start milking the cows.

Peter and his wife Mary have played at dances for many years. They live at Hellifield, but they could be anywhere in winter, keeping Dales feet lively, with Peter on the piano accordion and Mary keeping a brisk rhythm on the drums. I met Peter on a day when snow was being hurled at us by a wind full of spite. He was hoping they would not have to disappoint a faithful group of dancers at—Whitby.

My wife and I have danced to Beresford's Band many times at Austwick, where once, having two minutes' rest, we were approached by an old-timer who said: "Thou wants to git up an' shak thi supper down." Another band included a pianist, though the instrument was sluggish. Too many cups of tea had slithered into the open top.

The Boothman family of Linton-in-Craven help to keep the tradition of Dales dancing alive. Some of the dances being performed were among those collected in the 1930s by Lilian Douglas, of Giggleswick, and published with the music in two (now quite rare) books.

There's a jauntiness about Dales dancing. In an old-tyme waltz, an old farmer said to his partner: "Eh, luv, can you reverse?" She replied: "Are you getting dizzy?" He said: "Nay—but you're unscrewing me wooden leg."

Harry Cockerill, of Askrigg, will be remembered as an outstanding player of the piano accordion. He (like Peter Beresford) was self-taught. Harry told me: "I did my practising when I was a bachelor living by missen at High Greenfield, way beyond Beckermonds, which—you'll 'appen knaw—is t'source of the river Wharfe! At first, Harry travelled to dances on a motor bike, with his piano accordion strapped to the pillion seat.

I like my dancing well-organised, so that after a few twirls I can resort to automatic pilot and concentrate on talking to my partner. Gossip is the small change of Dales life. A Doris Waltz is just the thing. There's nothing simpler.

In a Progressive Barn Dance, you find yourself dancing with the long and the short and the tall, from gangling schoolgirls and young ladies wearing next-to-nowt, to old 'uns who were waltzing and fox-trotting before you were born. Sometimes you bruise your fingers on whalebone corsets.

Unless it's a special "do", supper consists of a cup of good Yorkshire tea and a plate with a couple of sandwiches and a bun. At Austwick, many moons ago, those serving tea at the Young Farmers' Club dance filled the cups of the dancers from a bucket. There's almost certainly an EEC regulation to prohibit that sort of thing today.

Not even an army of bureaucrats would be able to stop Dalesfolk and their friends from dancing to the strains of piano accordion, piano and drums. As an enthusiastic owd-time dancer says: ''It's t'best way of shortening the winter.''

Lambing Time on the Hill Farms

THE month-long lambing season demanded round-the-clock attention. The farmer or one of his sons cat-napped on the kitchen sofa, rising periodically to tour the lambing fields with a storm lantern. Now the heavily-pregnant ewes are driven into large sheds, where they might cheat the wind and weather. And any farmer with "brass" to chuck about might lig in bed and watch the happenings in the shed through the miracle of close-circuit television.

Over forty years ago, I courted a lass who lived on a farm which lies seven miles out of Skipton. At lambing time, if we went for a walk in the comparatively brief period between arrival at the farm and the last bus at 9 p.m., it was more than likely we'd have to leuk t'sheep as well. Afternoon tea (eaten in the glow of a paraffin lamp) might be interrupted by the appearance in the kitchen of my future father-in-law, bearing a chilled or ailing lamb he'd rescued from the elements. He would slip it into a well-lagged box at the fireside, or even into the oven, to warm up the lile creature. Nowadays, a starved (chilled) lamb is subjected to a hot blast from a hair-dryer.

If the chilled lamb was an orphan, or the mother ewe had no milk of her own, it was given a drink of cow's milk into which a hot poker had been plunged, thus complying with an old Dales tradition. For years, there was an idea that cow's milk which was not treated in this way was not suited to the digestive system of a sheep.

Some of t'owd timers, on their rounds of the lambing crofts, led a she-goat on a string, the animal being a ready source of rich milk at the right temperature. She-goats delivered their kids early in the year and when lambing was taking place on the hill farms had a good milk flow. At other times they made for the craggiest areas, such as Malham Cove, Kilnsey Crag or Trow Gill (near Clapham).

Accompanying Dad on his evening rounds, I saw him use his shepherd's crook with the speed of an adder's tongue to gather up lambs for attention. And I became familiar with the feel of a lamb's floppy, damp form and pounding heart as I carried a waif back to the farm for sanctuary, with t'owd ewe plodding bleatingly behind us.

In April, lambing time is in full swing at the upland farms. The contralto voices of the ewes are joined by the soprano hunger calls of new lambs. At a thousand feet above sea level, lambing is usually a chilling affair, with hail or sleet on the wind. They say that a good lamb is one that's roasted twice—yance on t'hill and yance in t'oven.

In this high-tech age, not much is left to chance—and nobody plunges a hot poker into the cow's milk to fill an orphan lamb's feeding bottle. The pregnant ewes are subjected to ultra-sound scanning of their wombs. The farmer knows in advance how many lambs to expect. He can separate the singles from the triplets and feed the sheep accordingly. What would his old grandfather have thought about this?

At lambing time, the basic routine is summed up by some short, sharp, typically Dales words—dip (the navel), strip (the colostrum from the ewe), sip (what the lamb does at the parental milk-bar) and clip (the tail). You will gather that there's, nowt glamorous about lambing time, especially when it's cold and wet or when a visiting crow, not content with dining on the afterbirth, has plucked the eyes from a weakly lamb while the mother concentrates on delivering a twin. A crow lags its nest with sheep wool. In Stockdale, near Settle, where nesting trees are few and far apart, crows nested on wall-tops.

Anthony Bradley, who was reared at Merebeck, between Long Preston and Settle, recalls a lambing time during the 1914-18 war when ice and snow sealed the land and it was necessary to put sheep and lambs under cover. Eventually, the only place which remained untenanted was the outside privy, known to a refined person as a toilet. A ewe and its lamb was bedded down here. And ever afterwards, that particular strain was known as "them privy sheep".

The National Farmers' Union organises "lamb banks" with an interchange of information about spare lambs available to be "mothered on" to bereaved ewes. A hand-reared lamb can be a nuisance, losing all fear of humans. Fred Bullock, who farmed at Barrel Sykes, near Settle, recalled a dipping-time when impulsively he decided to drop a pet lamb into the foul-smelling solution. Staggering from the dipping-trough, the lamb ran into the farmhouse living room—and shook itself before the fire!

The old Dales breeds were the Swardles (Swaledales) and Dales-breds, the first named type being fixed by farmers living on and around Tan Hill. The second breed originated in Upper Wharfedale, one of the founders being O Robinson, a Bradford wool merchant who was also a practical farmer in the dale.

A farmer whose living room window takes in a view of Penyghent has "just getten a few Beltex sheep. They're a mixture of Belgian and Texel. My old father would have called 'em 'fancy'." A Dales vet who shall be nameless calls a Beltex "thick and musclelly", adding "it looks as though it's collided with a wall."

All young life is appealing, even the Beltex, as you may see for yourself if you travel the Pennine daleheads and highroads just now.

Emblem of the National Park

ANYONE entering the Dales National Park by road sees a sign bearing the handsome head of Rastus the Ram, emblem of the Park. He has a black face, grey muzzle and massive horns which curve like the handlebars of a sports bike.

The emblem was drawn from a prize-winning tup of the Swaledale breed. Nature did the Dales farmer a good service by providing such headpieces as those splendid horns. As a Wensleydale man said, with the flicker of a smile: "Tha's summat to 'od on to when t'sheep's in an awk'ard mood."

The real-life Rastus was working overtime last autumn, which was tupping time in the hill farming calendar. Proof of his virility is to be seen everywhere in a fine crop of lambs. He also transmitted the characteristics of the Swaledale breed—a nice head, reasonable length of neck, a square body and four sound legs. One Dales breeder, long since gone to his rest, advised: "Allus mak sure the mouth and legs are all reight. A sheep uses 'em more than owt else."

Selling and buying tups is, according to a Hawes friend, "a hairy business". Quite apart from skill and judgement, you need a lot of luck. "One chap can make a fortune from selling tups. Another may buy at a high price and get poor results." A promising tup kept for breeding begins to cover ewes as a shearling (it has been shorn once). So a lamb born this spring will go to the tup sales in October next year.

The better quality animals sell for between £5,000 and £12,000. there was a one-off transaction at Kirkby Stephen, a prime centre for Swaledale sheep, in which the cost price was a staggering £48.000. Swaledale tups "as good as owt you'll find" are on view at the annual Tan Hill show towards the

end of May. The springtime weather on Tan Hill is "chancy".
Once it was cold—my body was wracked by six-inch shivers.
Another time, rain descended like water from a celestial
hosepipe. Sheep seem impervious to bad weather.

When Tan Hill is basking in sunshine, and larks ascend like
feathered helicopters, the highest licensed premises in the
land are packed with chattering farmfolk. T'Swardle tups—or
teearps in the local lingo—have their faces washed and their
fleeces "fluffed up" ready for judgement. Sometimes, sheep
are, indeed, "awk'ard" and dig in their sharp cleaves so that
the farmer or his lad has to drag an animal towards the ring
where the judges wait.

A retired farmer I met at the last Tan Hill Show told me:
"Before t'show season's finished, some o' yon sheep'll be
sick to death o' being handled. There's only one cure—stick
'em back on t'moor for a while till their eyes get their sparkle
back." At Tan Hill, I marvelled at the condition of the best
tups after an inclement winter. The farmer gave a brief
chuckle. "Them tups have been kept in t'parlour." They had
received the best attention and food.

It reminded me of one of Kit Calvert's stories relating to
Bob o' Cam, the nickname of Bob Lambert, who lived at
Camhouses, one of the cluster of remote farms near the
sources of Wharfe and Ribble. Bob really did keep tups in
t'parlour when he was expecting an intending buyer. Once,
during a trip to Hawes market, Bob was short of beer-money.
He saw a dealer trying to sell Model T Fords and, reckoning
that if he showed interest he would be offered a pint of ale,
Bob offered to buy a car "if tha can get it up to my farm." The
dealer said a Ford would go anywhere. He bought Bob a pint.
The car foundered up to its axles on the moor leading to
Camhouses.

Tups, like old soldiers, fade away. A tup mustn't cover its
own daughters. Some animals are sold for breeding; others
for killing. At the age of five or six years, Rastus the Dales
Ram is past his best. He may be remembered with pleasure

if his progeny are thriving and, in a practical form, if one of his horns has been considered good enough to form the headpiece of a shepherd's crook.

J B Priestley's Wharfedale

I RETURNED home on a spring day in 1965 to find my wife flustered. She had been baking and had floury hands. It was lunchtime and two small children, home from school, were at their noisy best. She intercepted me at the front door and whispered: "J B Priestley and Jacquetta Hawkes are waiting to see you."

And so they were. The Bradford-born wordsmith was sucking the stem of a pipe. Mercifully, he had not lit it or it would have poured out smoke like a West Riding mill with a rush-order for cloth.

The visit of almost thirty years ago was recalled when my wife and I had our annual springtime trip to the head of Wharfedale. We try to choose a day when winter and spring overlap—when daffodils bloom in the dale and patches of snow lie in the ancient joints of the hills.

My wife's maternal ancestors, the Bells, have strong territorial claims in the churchyards at Hubberholme and Aysgarth. Though not born in the Dales, J B Priestley would qualify to be a Honorary Dalesman and his ashes repose at Hubberholme, which he called "one of the smallest and pleasantest places in the world."

The centenary of Priestley's birth occurs this year. A brass plate on a pillar at the back of Hubberholme Church commemorates the Dales connection with this crotchety but lovable personality who wrote enduring prose. He was fascinated by dalesmen and observed: "Talking among themselves, they sound Scandinavian, rather like minor Ibsen characters." Luvly!

Why should Priestley and his wife have called unexpectedly to see us at Settle? He was writing an article for an

American magazine. A friend of ours, who had commissioned the piece, mentioned my connection with *The Dalesman*. He and Jacquetta called for a chat. They wandered off for a meal, having asked me to recommend a cafe, not a posh hotel. Curiosity led me to visit the cafe a few days later. It was pure Good Companions, down to the menu propped against a sauce bottle. On the menu was the item: "Plumbs and Custard".

While Jacquetta went to Victoria Cave, I took Priestley to Tot Lord's Pigyard Club museum and its array of bones and artefacts connected wsith the skin-clad, harpoon-toting earliest Dales residents. I suggested that to understand these bits of bone, horn and enamelled ornaments, one should try to get into the mind of Early Man. Priestley boomed: "The salvation of the human race is in getting OUT of the mentality of Early Man."

He truly loved the Dales. When after the trauma of service in the 1914-18 war, he returned to civilian life, he persuaded the Editor of the *Yorkshire Observer* to use a series of articles from him based on a walking tour of the region. He had thus walked "out of the iron and blood and misery of war into worldland, still magically illuminated by memories of my boyhood." Priestley told me there were four or five articles, for which he was paid "a guinea a time".

In his book English Journey (published in 1934), he mentioned a daleswoman who stopped visiting Kettlewell (not the noisiest place on earth) because, as she explained to a friend, "I can't stand t'racket."

Dick Chapman, of Bainbridge, taught him how to catch crayfish. Dick, who also had Bradford connections, was a man Priestley loved to meet. He "belongs to my generation and has all its fiery energy and optimism." Priestley enjoyed chatting with Marie Hartley and Joan Ingilby, the Dales historians, at their home in Askrigg.

Marie photographed him hard at work by the Ingleton-Hawes road painting an impression (in gouache) of Ingleborough, the "big blue hill". He painted only when he was on holiday "and"—as he told me—"I get very cross when I can't do it." We had the pleasure of reproducing his Ingleborough study in *The Dalesman.*

My last Dales meeting with J B Priestley was when I arranged to interview him at the Rose and Crown in Bainbridge, where he loved to stay. It was a calm, sunny morning. At the appointed time, I stood outside the inn, listening to the machine-gun pattern of his typewriter and seeing wraiths of pipe smoke emerge from a half-opened window to join the cumulous clouds in the sky.

He leaned out of the window and re-arranged the appointment. We would meet at Muker later in the morning. He arrived on time, wearing his beret and, of course, sucking the stem of his pipe. He loved the music of his friend Elgar who, incidentally, was another great pipe-smoker.

Priestley spent the last twenty years of his life at Kissing Tree House, Alveston, in the Shakespeare Country. Tot Lord, of Settle, once visited him there "on spec" with "something" wrapped in a grubby piece of newspaper. "Nay, I thought you'd like to see this, Mr Priestley," said Tot, removing the paper to reveal a valuable medieval book he had borrowed from a friend.

Priestley was not religious in the orthodox sense, yet in April, 1986, by special faculty, his ashes were buried in the churchyard at Hubberholme. He had written about the Dales churchyards that they are "crowded with the tombstones of people who died in their late eighties. These lives were saved by air fit to breathe, food fit to eat and the challenge of wild weather."

Priestley had come back to his beloved Dales. He would have been wryly amused if he could have known that before interment his ashes, in their casket, would be stored for a few weeks under the stairs of a local house.

A Dipper Casts its Own Spell

THE DIPPER, a water-sprite found on the unpolluted hill becks of the Dales, is at home where Janet's Foss tumbles into a clear, cold plunge pool within easy walking distance of Malham.

Janet is said to have been the queen of the local fairies who occupied a hole behind the waterfall. So if you see a wee creature with a crumpled ballet dress, bedraggled wings and a dirty wand, you known where to find her lodgings.

In contrast with a dishevelled fairy, the dipper is always neat and tidy. Its very existence depends on how well it maintains its drip-dry plumage for, unique among British birds, this water-sprite collects its food—larvae and other tit-bits—during a walkabout on the bed of a beck or river.

Janet's Foss is a magical spot, being a little gorge bedecked with ash and hazel. In spring, there is continuous noise from a rookery (which a young friend calls a "croakery") and the humid atmosphere around Janet's Foss is ideal for the growth of mosses and ferns. Look out for the hooded flowers of the cuckoo-pint which will develop into spikes with scarlet berries.

Recently, I sat just above the Foss, drinking thermos-coffee and peering at an acute angle into the clear beck, which blends its water with another watercourse, half a mile below Malham, to form the River Aire. A submerged dipper walked into view, moving upstream. So clear was the water, I might have been peering through glass. There was nothing to distort the bird's shape. Strong feet grasped the rocks. The plumage was not black, as it appears from a distance, but an attractive chocolate-brown. The dipper has a prominent white "bib".

Charles Kingsley, a gentle Hampshire clergyman, and author of *The Water-Babies,* a Victorian classic, must have seen dippers in this district while staying at Malham Tarn House. (Kingsley knew the Dales quite well, having ecclesiastical connections with Middleham in Wensleydale). Perhaps, in Malhamdale, he was aware of the special view of the bird to be obtained where water races and bubbles just above Janet's Foss.

I see at least one dipper when I have my regular early morning walk. I cross the dipper-haunted Ribble twice—at Langcliffe Locks and Settle Bridge. The bird has a strong sense of territory. When the young of one brood have been reared to independence, they are sent on their way. Dippers are usually double-brooded. I saw a dipper pair feeding their slate-grey young which were well-spread, perched on stones in mid-river. The young were lighter in shade than their parents, but the dumpy, wren-like shape was unmistakable.

Dippers are nervous in human company, yet when David Binns, the bird artist, and I went for a walk with a Yorkshire TV film crew for a sequence in *The Dales Diary,* a local dipper not only stayed on its favourite boulder but went through a vigorous preening routine as well. More recently, out with filmsters connected with the Natural History Unit of the BBC, I saw one on the water-washed boulders as the camera and other equipment was assembled. Entertainment was provided by the local dippers, one of which allowed such a close approach, without so much as a blink, we began to entertain the idea it had been left by a taxidermist.

Arthur Gilpin, a veteran field naturalist, recalled a December day when the water between the pebbles of a Dales shingle bank was turning to ice. He saw three dippers. It was the classic triangle drama. From their postures, and from their rippling, chizzicking songs, it was soon evident that two males were displaying to each other. One of them would have to go...and did, with the local bird in noisy pursuit.

Both cock and hen dippers give a warbling song. At other times, I hear a metallic flight call, zit, zit, as a nervous bird departs at speed. The sharp sound it pitched high. It is distinguishable from the tumultuous sound of the river.

The pure water of the Wharfe at Bolton Abbey is dipper-friendly. At Clapham, in the days when I regularly crossed t'Brokken Bridge on my way to the post office, I would see

the local dipper doing the avian equivalent of press-ups before wading or plunging into the beck to feed. In shallow places, I traced its progress by watching the ripples from its exposed back.

Many nests are built under bridges or in culverts. A favourite nesting place in my district is on a ledge provided by one of the metal girders supporting a footbridge. A nest made at the side of a Pennine waterfall had been used so often it was composed of living moss, though within the structure was an inner cup, lined with leaves which remained dry. Seeing a startled dipper appear from beneath a single-span bridge in the lead-mining country of Swaledale led me to look under the bridge. I admired the workmanship not only of a pair of nest-building dippers but of the human bridge-builders who, in the middle of last century, raised an arch which stands firmly to this day.

The most astonishing dipper nest I recorded this year was a depression on a mossy boulder in the middle of the Skir-fare, the river of Littondale. On a springtime jaunt, when bird-life was profuse, I put up pairs and small groups of oystercatchers, no less than fifty birds in all. A pair of goosanders shot the rapids.

Then I noticed a dipper, with nesting material in its beak, alight on the boulder and make its way to a moss-fringed hole, from which its mate appeared and flew off. Dippers are faithful to nesting sites where they have not been unduly disturbed. From the mossy state of the boulder I judged it was not often overswept by the river.

In any case, fledged young take readily to water. A friend saw a young dipper lose its footing and fall into the river. Without undue fuss, although it called to attract attention, this Dales water-sprite spread its wings on the water and floated with the current until it reached a landing place.

An Unlikely Television Star

OVER TWENTY years ago, as we discussed a Saturday jaunt in the Dales, my wife said: "I've never visited Tan Hill. Nor have I had a chat with Hannah Hauxwell." We promptly turned the bonnet of the car towards the high Pennines.

Hannah, a television celebrity, was known to be "a late getter-up". We had a bar-snack at Tan Hill inn, the highest licensed premises in England, before driving to Baldersdale, the quiet tributary valley of the Tees which was home to Miss Hauxwell. Using a winding track between "rush-bobs", under the steely gaze of horned sheep, we arrived at Low Birk Hatt, beside a huge reservoir which Hannah called "my Mississippi".

A knock on the door brought the sound of yapping from a terrier-type dog. We heard Hannah rebuking it for its bad manners. Ere long, we were chatting with a daleswoman in her early sixties who, though silver-haired, had the rosy complexion of someone who regularly washed in beck water and did not resort to cosmetics. She used a beck which flowed in the field at the back of her house; if the flow ceased, in summer, she could always resort to the reservoir...

We were impressed by her charm. Television pictures had prepared us for the scrow (untidy appearance) of her living room. Hannah lived alone, had a smallholding and some recalcitrant cattle to maintain. There was little time to spare for housework. Said Hannah, with a grin: "I think I was born in a pickle." In the room were two long-case clocks made by a long-dead craftsman at Barnard Castle, a paraffin lamp for emergencies, a stone jar of the type which once held home-made beer (doubtless made specially for haytime) and parcels

35

neatly tied up using binder twine, the Dales farmer's best friend.

I noticed a head-and-shoulder photograph of grandmother, clad in bonnet and Sunday-best gown. She looked no different from scores of other stern-faced Dales grandmothers who, when photographed in a dim studio by plate-camera, had been told by the photographer not to smile or the image would blur.

Hannah, during the short cloudy summers and long, wearying winters, craved for sunshine. As she remarked: "In summer I live; in winter, I exist." It became a custom for us, when on holiday, to send Hannah a picture postcard of somewhere basking under an azure sky. As the years went by, Hannah began to tell us of her own travels, each trip leading up to a television documentary and eventually to a whole series. Now WE had cause to be envious. She was taken to a garden party at Buckingham Palace, where she saw the Queen, though at a distance, and had "brown bread and butter, a lovely little pancake, a cheese scone, a piece of fruit cake and some chocolate cake. Being me, I had TWO cups of tea.

Knowing she was partial to sponge cake, and had little time to make any, we usually baked her one and my wife performed the difficult task of carrying it across country to the farm. Once, when Hannah was raking hay in the top meadow— wearing Great Auntie's bonnet to shade her face—she thanked us for the cake and asked us to leave it under an upturned calf bucket, near the back door, where her dog could not reach it.

Hannah has no romantic ideas about life on a Dales farm in t'owd days. Of a haytime of the 1930s, she said: "It was a tough, slogging time. We were always understaffed. One bad haytime we 'packed in' on November 17. Then we hadn't got it all." Even on Christmas Day she was absorbed by "beast-work". She would remark: "I wish it was always summer."

A television documentary recorded her "flitting" from Low Birk Hatt to Cotherstone, a few miles away. When we called to see her at her new home, I noticed that the case of one of her clocks had been fettled-up using—er, yes—the ubiquitous binder twine. On the farm, Hannah had been quite an artist with such twine, especially when it came to repairing gates. We next saw the clock among the items photographed for a television series in which celebrities had to guess from a filmed sequence whose house it was. In Hannah's case, they failed. To anyone who knew her, the twine-fettled clock was unmistakable.

Hannah has become quite a gadabout (as the Dalesfolk say). She enjoys her jaunts. We meet now and again when I interview her at some charity event. She is not a public speaker as such, but talks freely when questioned. She does not like to know the questions in advance. We were "on the programme" at a small chapel where 104 people had assembled for an old-style Dales meeting. With seating for 100, the chairman was among those who sat on the floor. We were entertained as well as inspired by Edwin and John Coates, two of Hannah's chapel friends from Teesdale, who sang the old-time hymns and choruses. Hannah responded, mouthing the words and tapping her feet.

Hannah's weak eyesight means that she shuns bright lights. When signing books, she writes with a felt-point pen, in huge letters—almost like sign-writing—and adds the date. As in all things, she does not hurry, ordering her life by the old Dales dictum that if a job's worth doing—it's worth doing well.

I asked her about her daily routine. She hadn't one! Hannah confessed to being no better at getting out of bed than she had been at Low Birk Hatt. She smiled, then added: "Me and time do not go well together."

Chapters in a Dales Life

JUST sixty years ago, Ella Pontefract and Marie Hartley, of Wetherby, formed a writer and artist partnership, rented a disused farmhouse at Angram and gathered material for a book about Swaledale life and traditions.

Ella wrote in her diary that they were staying at "a funny rambling old house with all the windows facing the wrong way." Marie recalls: "When we wanted a bath, we were loaned a tin one, on the understanding that it was returned every Saturday so that Tom, our landlady's youngest child, might have his weekly bath."

Swaledale, published by Dent in 1934, was written by Ella, who had recently studied folklore at University College, London. It was illustrated by Marie, who had tuition in painting from the artist Owen Bowen and in wood-engraving from E Owen Jennings. Marie progressed from the Leeds College of Art to the Slade.

In 1938, having compiled books on Wensleydale and Wharfedale, they bought Coleshouse, a cottage at Askrigg. How they adapted it to their needs was told in the book *Yorkshire Cottage.* Ella died in 1946 at the age of forty-eight. Two years later, Joan Ingilby—herself a poet and writer—joined Marie at her Dales home. In 1968, Leeds University conferred on Marie an honorary MA. Marie (and Joan) themselves made a handsome gift of their collection of Dales bygones to the Dales Museum at Hawes.

Coleshouse, by the hill road leading from Askrigg into Swaledale, is an unpretentious Dales cottage, built of local materials and fittingly adapted to be the home of writer and artist. Nothing seemed to have changed since my last visit. The wrought-iron gate shut with a clunk, not a clatter. The garden was spangled with celandines. A burst of sunshine burnished the well-polished door-knocker.

Marie opened the door. The tradition of Dales hospitality was continued by Joan, who offered me a cup of coffee. We sat beside a coal fire, reminiscing about the Dales. It was at this fireside that J B Priestley had relaxed during a four days' stay with Marie and Joan. Television had reached the dale, but they rarely switched it on. Courtesy demanded that when Priestley revealed a fondness for televised boxing, he was allowed to watch a match. As the fight progressed, he gave a running commentary.

Now, Marie gave a brief commentary on the events sixty years before, when she and Ella had rented a farmhouse to research their Swaledale book. There was not a drop of rain for the whole month. Returning to the valley for a shorter period in October, they completed the work on what is now a classic study of a Yorkshire Dale.

They followed the success of *Swaledale* with a similiar study of Wensleydale and, having little spare cash, they operated from a second-hand caravan they had purchased at Otley. The van, named Green Plover, after the lapwing, a familiar Dales bird, was first driven to Shaw Paddock, near the source of the Ure and not far from the busy Settle-Carlisle railway. Each evening, as the two women went to their beds, a regular steam-hauled express thundered by.

Wharfedale completed a trilogy of outstanding books. Ella's death ended the collaboration, but the memory lingers on through her diary and published work. In the very first issue of *The Yorkshire Dalesman* she wrote about Dalesfolk and quoted a hill farmer, a man with the simple but strong faith of his ancestors: ''If there's another Noah's flood, there won't be many folk left alive i' England when t'watter comes bashin' down oor chimney pots.''

Marie's collaboration with Joan Ingilby, who lived at North Deighton, three miles from Wetherby, has led to the compilation of many more Dales books. Marie has albums of photographs of Dales life dating back to the 1930s. Theirs is a true collaboration. They write a chapter each; then exchange the chapters for criticism and revision. Marie told me: "I am best at the broad sweep of a book. Joan is a stickler for detail. We accept each other's criticism in the right spirit and work in perfect harmony."

To own a Dales cottage and live by writing is an attractive idea. Most of those who have tried to realise this dream failed, wrongly believing that such a life can be an extensive holiday in pleasant surroundings. Marie and Joan disciplined themselves when recording and writing about the life of their native Yorkshire.

There is much work yet to be done.

The Man Who Created Herriotshire

GOOD WISHES to Alf Wight (alias James Herriot), as the best-known Dales vet recovers from a close encounter with trespassing sheep. They had invaded the garden at his home which frames a view of the Hambleton Hills, east of Thirsk. He tried to turn the sheep from his flower beds. A stampede of errant animals left Herriot sprawled on the ground, nursing a broken left leg.

It was good to see him on television recently, in the company of Simon Ward, who played the part of Herriot when the book *All Creatures Great and Small* was filmed for the cinema a quarter of a century ago. This film was the precurser of a long-running BBC television series, introduced, each week of the run, by a "shot" of a 1930s saloon car on a road across the fells (Low Row to Langthwaite) and a hump-backed bridge (Langthwaite, near Reeth). Remember the jingling tune?

I include the placenames for the benefit of anyone in search of the Herriot haunts. Just now, in high summer, that part of the Dales which the tourist industry has dubbed Herriotshire sees a steady flow of pilgrims, many of whom have read the books. The others have joyful memories of the BBC series.

Alf Wight, OBE, is still quiet and self-effacing despite the international success of his books, which have sold by the million. He has not lost interest in the veterinary practice at Thirsk, where his son Jim is a vet and Donald Sinclair—the real-life Siegfried Farnon of the Herriot books—an occasional visitor.

Astonishingly, Herriot's writing career began when he was

turned fifty (and had celebrated the silver anniversary of his wedding). He was chivvied by his wife into putting down some of the interesting tales he used to recount when returning from a work-trip in the Dales and which one day would be included in his book. When the writing urge could not be ignored, this busy vet made time in the evening. Every line of the best-sellers was jotted down in the living room, while sitting before the television. The famous pen-name was adopted when, watching a televised football match, he noticed that the Birmingham goal-keeper was called James Herriot.

How did Alf Wight come to know the Dales? He told me of days spent helping Frank Bingham, an Irish vet, who had a large upper Dales practice based on Leyburn, in Wensleydale. It was a good time in which to work. In the 1930s and 1940s, before the onset of wonder-drugs, the old farmers occasionally practised a sort of black-magic to cure their stock. Such as tying up a goat in a shippon where there had been contageous abortion.

Herriot became fascinated by these hill farmers—"a race apart, proud, independent, spirited". And then he fell under the charm of the Dales landscape, which was not always bare and austere. One evening, after crossing the high road from Askrigg to Grinton, he stopped the car at the moor-edge to let out the dog. And he stared, with enchantment at the view of the lower valley of the Swale, with its fields, walls, barns and wooded hillsides, curving on its way to Richmond.

For many, the characters and authentic stories of the old Dales way of life are the compelling features of the Herriot books. I asked an old friend, Anthony Bradley, of Settle, for some information about Dales farming in the "thirties". He replied: "Read Herriot." We recall a hard, abrasive Dales farmer who had a bull suffering from sunstroke. The man was relieved that the treatment was not some fancy potion but water, played on the animal from a hose. It was *his* water, of course, so the vet could not in decency charge too much!

The owner of a pig with a boil on his face must have derived wry amusement from the unsuccessful attempts to capture the ferocious animal for treatment. It was left to Tristan, the younger brother of Siegfried, to effect the cure—by losing his temper and chasing the pig in darkness, causing it to brush against a wall and burst the boil.

The pilgrims of 1994 who set off in their cars and on their bikes for the Herriot Country should make not only for Swaledale (which, I fancy, is Alf Wight's favourite valley) and Wensleydale but also for the tributary valleys of Wensleydale—for Raydale, Bishopdale, Walden and Coverdale.

Richmondshire District Council, based on Richmond, acquired the "set" of Herriot's surgery as seen by television viewers; it is now a major feature of the Richmondshire Museum. The Council has also published a leaflet, *The Herriot Trail*, which is described as "a scenic drive around Wensleydale and Swaledale taking in locations from *All Creatures Great and Small*. It is recalled that between 1978 and 1983, forty-nine episodes of the BBC television series were broadcast.

Darrowby, the principal town in the books, is a composite place, having in it traces of Richmond, Middleham, Leyburn and Thirsk. Herriot also brought to bear his considerable imagination. The real Skeldale House of the veterinary practice is at Thirsk, but the BBC filmsters used a Cringley House, one of the Georgian houses in the centre of Askrigg, Wensleydale. At Carperby, near Aysgarth, the local inn has a plaque outside mentioning that this was where the real-life vet and his wife spent their honeymoon, having been married at Thirsk.

And, if you would picnic near the watersplash which the car negotiates in the opening sequence of every television film, go to Low Row in Swaledale and take the high road—in a literal sense—to near the remains of Surrender Smelt Mill. Beyond here, the road through the heatherland, between grouse and sheep with eyes as ancient-looking as the rocks, is crossed by a lively beck before making its final effort to the skyline and the descent to Langthwaite in Arkengarthdale.

In a world torn by strife, and at a time when so-called entertainment on television simply adds to our feelings of foreboding, Herriot restores to us something of our old faith in humanity.

A Dales Spring

HORTON-IN-RIBBLESDALE

We welcomed the many cheerful pink-kneed cyclists, solo and tandem; and still more we welcomed the stout-booted, rucksacked walkers, old and young—the smiling pilgrims of our hills and valleys.

John Dower, at Kirkby Malham (1941).

The Yorkshireman is proverbially proud of his county, and if his hills are not "in the run" among British mountains, they at all events cover plenty of ground...

Harry Speight (1895).

There is sound, too, on the fells; the angry clacking of grouse, the liquid pipe of curlews in the distance, "see-o-weet, see-o-weet" as a plover sweeps above...and the anxious calls of sheep and lambs.

Ella Pontefract, Swaledale (1934).

While brooding her nine or ten eggs, the hen grouse does not often leave the nest. Research using miniscule radio sets fixed to selected birds indicate that the time spent off the nest ranges from two to fifteen per cent. It depends on a bird's condition, which in turn is influenced by the quality of the heather and disease levels. Eggs on the lower moors hatch on about May 15, those on the higher moors hatching about the 22nd. The process is well synchronised and all the young birds of a brood emerge within twenty-four hours.

At Home with the Red Grouse

SPRING is tardy on the Pennines. When conditions are Spring-like far down the dale, winter maintains its grip on the moor. From the north-east comes snow. The east wind is cold, drying, sweeping the already impoverished heather and shrivelling it. Where the ling has been destroyed, brown patches are seen.

The few creatures which stir on the moors during the lean days move between the cores of old snowdrifts. The red grouse is among them. This astonishing bird remains faithful to its open, windswept Calluna moorland. In winter it has little company—just the crow, wren and high-stepping fox. At the approach of Spring, the waders return, with golden plover on the plateaux and lapwings in tumbling flight over the marginal ground.

My interest in the red grouse is not sporting but purely one of respect for a tough and characterful bird—an island variant of the willow grouse of far-northern scrublands. The willow grouse dons a white plumage for the winter. Our grouse stay dark, though if you were to look closely you might see a few white spots hinting at the bird's ancestry. The willow grouse does not attain such a high density as the red grouse. It is also smaller—and is perhaps not so good to eat.

The red grouse clings, in winter and summer alike, to its own patch of Pennine moorland. This bird is a prisoner on the moor through its dependence on heather for food. The grouse plucks heather shoots with a short bill which has the nip of a pair of secateurs. The bird has a gut especially adapted for dealing with fibrous plant food. A thick plumage affords insulation against the cold and wet. The feet of the stubby grouse are feathered. It gives the impression of wearing avian spats.

Kowa! kowa! kowa! The alarm call rouses the moorland echoes. In the air, the bird moves like a feathered missile, hugging the contours at a speed which attains sixty miles an hour—more if there is wind assistance.

Much of my knowledge of grouse is derived from chats with Dr Peter Hudson, who from a base at Askrigg in Wensleydale, carried out important studies for The Game Conservancy. I met Fennel, his pointer, who located the grouse chicks. I was shown one of the diminutive radio transmitters fitted to a grouse to keep a check on its movements.

Neville Turner, a veterinary surgeon in Teesdale, shares my admiration for the red grouse as a living creature adapted to life in a treeless area a thousand feet or more above sea level. Winter lasts eight months and you should not be surprised if, on midsummer day, a snowflake settles on your nose. When the moor is sealed by snow encrusted with ice, the dispirited grouse huddle on wall-tops near farms and villages. I met an old Wharfedale 'keeper who, as a lad, was sent to the moor to "bray" the snow with a besom and expose heather as food for the starving grouse.

Neville "shoots" grouse using a camera which has a lens like the barrel of a howitzer. Because his veterinary practice includes moorland roads, he is every alert for a photo-opportunity. His portraits of grouse show the cock bird's be-wattled head; a large clear eye (ringed by white) and a short horny beak which is well adapted to dealing with tough heather food. A glossy rufous-brown plumage offers a cock grouse splendid camouflage. The hen bird, lighter in tone, looks yellowish in her spring breeding plumage—if you can pick her out as she sits like a feathered tea-cosy in a jumble of moorland plants.

Early in the year, the grouse are helped into breeding condition by feeding on the flowers of the moss-crop, which is also a prime food plant for sheep. The hen grouse needs plenty of nourishment to enable her to produce a clutch of eleven eggs (in early April) and to sit on them for about 27 days. After grouse have mated, the hen makes her nest, usually in heather which is a foot or so high. There is no help from the cock bird, though he does mount sentry duty.

Grouse chicks (hatched out in late May) are precocious, lively from the point of hatching and soon trying to use their stumpy wings. Spring storms batter and chill any young grouse which are caught in the open. A dry season reduces the extent of the sphagnum bogs where it is vital for the growing chicks to take in protein-rich insect food. They soon grow a special gut which is capable of dealing with fibrous heather. Who'd be a grouse? A chick may become host to a tick, which will suck its blood or carry the lethal virus of louping-ill. Some birds are afflicted by the parasitic Strongyle threadworm, which damages the lining of the gut.

If a grouse survives the chick stage; if it grows up to evade the sportsman's shot in August, then its life expectancy is probably two and a-half years. To reach that age is remarkable considering the bleak environment, the pressures against the nesting bird, the rigours of winter and the hungry period as winter gives way to spring.

Up in Swaledale, last century, the Cherry family attempted to restore order and a grouse stock to moorland which had been heavily poached by miners and visited by the notorious Weardale Gang. Matthew Cherry told me his grandfather spent many a moonlit night listening for poachers. It was said that because lead-miners worked in semi-darkness they had especially good night eyes.

As a boy, Matthew was taught how to call grouse. Sitting in a hollow or behind a wall at first light in November—when older birds pair—he would imitate the call of a hen bird and attract the swaggering moorcocks. Grandfather had a wooden smoker's pipe with which he could call grouse.

My own feeble efforts are restricted to trying to imitate the alarm call—*Kowa! kowa! kowa!*—in March. The nearest grouse are more likely to be perplexed than anxious.

Last of the "Terrible" Knitters

THE DRUMMY sound of clogs against cobbles in the main street of Dent drew attention to Betty Hartley, clad in Victorian garb, who was knitting on her way to visit her good friend Elizabeth Middleton. They carry on the tradition of the "terrible knitters 'e Dent".

Hand-knitting as a means of eking out a pittance earned in farming was practised in several Yorkshire dales, from Dentdale to Swaledale, and in some of the Westmorland dales as well. At Gayle, near Hawes, Brian Alderson told me that his 18th century cotton mill was once used for processing wool for Dales hand-knitters. Gayle Mill was recently scheduled as an Ancient Monument.

We recall the Dent knitters because Southey, in a novel called *The Doctor,* used the memorable expression "terrible knitters 'e Dent". That word terrible does not mean shoddy but "great". Almost ceaseless knitting was not an amusing diversion. It was hard work. When the weekly delivery of wool was made by cart from Kendal—it began at the end of the eighteenth century and lasted for about ninety years—there was an urge to knit stockings, jerseys, mittens and gloves to supplement a miserable income on the little upland farms.

As James Walton, who studied Dales crafts, wrote, hand-knitting at Dent was "a task cold and hard like the granite masses which surround the village and impart their stubborn, dour character to the natives themselves." The coarsely spun wool brought by the weekly cart was known as "bump", and a bump-knitter rocked backwards and forwards (also crooning a song) as her nimble fingers handled the four curved, metal needles. One needle was slipped into

50

a hole at the end of a dagger-like knitting stick (known in other parts of the Dales as a sheath) which was held firm by a leather belt.

William Howitt (1844) wrote of Dent knitters who sat "rocking to and fro like so many weird wizards. They burn no candle but knit by the light of the peat fire. And this rocking motion is connected with a mode of knitting peculiar to the place, called swaying..." The Dent knitting stick is a collectable antique. Some good examples may be seen in Yorkshire museums. Many sticks were made locally, some for young men who were courting; a suitor handed a stick to his lady-love as a love token (or maybe to hint at what was to be expected of her when they were married and needed to earn a living).

Betty Hartley's grand progress up the cobbled street at Dent in old-time clothes was staged for a television film, though she and Miss Middleton have given numerous demonstrations of the craft, dressing up for added authenticity and talking or singing the old Dent songs as they plied the needles. It was fascinating to watch a cameraman walking beside Mrs Hartley and holding the camera close to her beclogged feet. A sound-recordist followed, putting on magnetic tape the distinctive *clump, clump* of the "irons" against rounded stones.

I recalled that I first saw the two Dentdale knitters when the Settle-Carlisle railway centenary was being celebrated in 1976. A special train drew up beside the "down" platform at Dent, which is the highest mainline station in Britain. Theoretically it was spring but rain was being hurled at us by a wind full of spite. Ice cream was on offer. There were few takers. The "hand-knitters" stood out because each had donned a lace-fringed cap, long gown and fancy shawl.

I asked Betty Hartley when she first knitted in the special Dent way. Her mother had taught her how to knit when she was three years old. Betty has a stick which was made by William Oversby, her grandfather. At one time (she added) virtually everyone in the dale knitted. Her grandfather had done this while sitting at the front of a horse-drawn cart on his way to Dent railway station to collect a load of coal.

There was something satisfying in being allowed to handle a knitting stick which had been used for many years. It was shaped like the wing of a goose. A ledge along the widest part prevents the stick from slipping behind the leather belt which held it against the knitter's body. A cylindrical haft had a hole burnt into it and was reinforced by a brass ring to prevent it slipping. This hole was to hold one of the needles.

The two ladies use Arran wool, which is "as near as we can get to the original type. . .In the old days, the wool was thick and oily, also dirty and rather smelly. A lot of stockings were made for use with seamen's boots; lots of them were exported to Russia." In the heyday of Dales hand-knitting, a pair of stockings was knitted for a shilling, which was also the payment received for "one of the beautiful Dent gloves."

Mrs Sedgwick, a native of Dent who spent her later years in Settle, used to tell me about her knitting-stick, which was made by the local joiner and was in use before she began to attend school. She showed me the knitting tackle and sportingly (despite her age and arthritis) knitted a row or two.

I asked Mrs Hartley who she considered to be the last of the "terrible knitters"? It was possibly Polly Stephenson, "who was an old lady when I was a girl." Polly lived with her parents at Flintergill, Dent, and they all knitted commercially.

The need to meet commercial deadlines is over. Modern Dent knitters are engaged in the craft for pleasure—even for fun!

Re-discovering the High Dales

ABOUT four million Britons go walking for pleasure. In the Dales we see one of the hardier types - the fell-walker, doing his or her steady two miles an hour, indifferent to the terrain.

Forty years ago, I stood with a Dales farmer at Grinton, in Swaledale, as three young lads walked briskly by, protecting themselves against the rain with simple waterproof capes, of the type issued to soldiers during the war. They were shod in ex-Army boots. The farmer, amazed that anyone should walk for pleasure, commented: "Hevvn't you chaps getten homes to go to?"

Today, fell-walkers arrive by the bus load and swarm up the popular peaks in multi-coloured splendour. The lads I saw at Grinton would be heading for the moor-edge youth hostel, which had some of the grandeur of a castle and was then being wardened by my good friends, Ron and Lucie Hinson.

The 1930s were a depressing time industrially. They also saw the re-discovery, on the cheap, of the English countryside. Walkers and cyclists living in industrial towns, where the factory chimneys had stopped smoking, suddenly became aware of natural beauty and clean skies in an area like the Dales. Youth hostelling, which began in Germany, soon spread to this country. The now-familiar green triangle of the YHA appeared in the most popular places. A walking or cycling tour could be planned using a different hostel each night. At Aysgarth, hostellers were entertained by Mr Gummerson and his "talking" dog which, when it was not talking, had a smoker's pipe in its mouth!

Another triangle had upon it the initials CTC, representing

the Cyclists' Touring Club. Call at a farmhouse displaying this sign, and you might have a cup of tea and some cake for a few coppers. And a few coppers more secured a bed for the night. When travelling in the Dales, on foot or bike, it was as well to have "summat to eit" at regularly intervals or you might have a debilitating attack of hunger-knock. Mrs Brown, of Malham Post Office, made claggy fruit cake which kept the hunger-pangs at bay.

Old-time walkers wore their most durable clothes, had boots (complete with studs) on their feet, packed a few sandwiches and (if they were wealthy) had a thermos flask. Mrs Mason of Gayle, near Hawes, recalls that her mother, on a trip to Liverpool early in the century, returned with a thermos, the first to be seen in Wensleydale.

On a bitterly cold Spring day, when the sheep were being driven from winter grazings in Wharfedale, over Fleet Moss to their home farms, mother suggested a hot drink would not go amiss. The flask was filled. Mrs Mason—then a young lass—saddled up her pony and took it to the men as they slithered down from the Moss. The first one to drink gulped from the thermos—and spent the rest of the day trying to cool down his throat. The heat of the liquid had taken him completely by surprise.

Today, with thermoses and dehydrated food, you might make a five-course meal on Buckden Pike. On my last visit to the summit of Cross Fell, at around 3,000 ft the "attic" of the Pennines, I arrived at mid-morning to find the still hot ashes from a fire where some walkers had (doubtless enjoyed) a barbecued breakfast. Sitting by the waterfall in Posforth Gill, Bolton Abbey, I was in the course of transferring a Scotch egg to my mouth when a hungry pheasant flew at me. I warded off the bird with my plastic lunch box. The Scotch egg rolled down a slope into the beck.

A trickle of fell-walkers has become a flood. The procession is like a fashion parade, each walker wearing a colourful, well-tailored outfit, with boots and gaiters and gargantuan rucksacks. At Horton-in-Ribblesdale, a native's jaw drooped with astonishment on seeing a bus-load of expensively-attired walkers: "They must have hundreds o' quid's worth o' tackle on their backs," he declared.

The old name for rucksack was "haversack", originally a little bag in which the old Scottish cattle-drovers carried their oatmeal, with which to make haverbread. The drovers travelled light. Old Abraham Banks, of Malham Moor, used to say that if a hungry drover was in a hurry he made a small hole in t'grund, mixed oatmeal with water, ate what he wanted and let his dog lick out the hole.

Fell-walkers are well-organised. Once, while doing the Three Peaks, I met two young men—and one rucksack. They had arranged that each would carry it for half an hour at a time. A Londoner who was airing his multi-blistered feet was applying "Germaline and sheep's wool". Where fell-walkers meet, they discuss achievements. Some have completed the Pennine Way, plodding through peat and along eroded paths for 250 miles from Edale in Derbyshire to Kirk Yetholm in Scotland. Others are veterans of The Dales Way, from Ilkley to Bowness, which passes through a leafy wonderland by the Strid.

Having researched the fifty year long friendship between the composer Edward Elgar and a Giggleswick doctor, Charles William Buck, I related some Elgarian references in his letters to local places and devised The Elgar Way, which I first walked in the company of Betty Wainwright (wife of the best-known fell-walker) and my old walking friend, Bob Swallow.

I then walked it with a lively nonegenarian from Addingham. He had an aversion to sitting down. When, after a few miles, I reached for my sandwiches, he remarked: "I hope we're not going to spend too much time eating."

That's the fell-walking spirit!

The Shorthorn:
A Dalesman's Cow

AFTER TEA, the farmer living at the edge of Malham Moor slurred his chair on the flagged floor of the kitchen, rose a little wearily to his feet (for the pre-tea sleep-mist was still upon him), collected a paraffin lamp and announced that he was "bahn to milk". I followed him into a tiny shippon where, sitting on the traditional three-legged stool, with the pail between his knees, he turned the neb of his cap to the back and pressed his head against the flank of a cow, which he described as a "strawberry roan".

There were few sounds beyond the steady hiss of the lamp and the swish of milk against the side of the pail as he coaxed milk from the cow's teats by rhythmic movements of his fingers. As the level of the milk rose, it was obscured by froth. It was (said the farmer) a good cow to milk, not a "short-papped 'un"...I'd one cow 'at started sprayin' out milk as soon as it heard t'proven bucket."

The scene in that little shippon was half as old as life in the Dales. The boskins (wooden partitions between the stalls) were smooth and polished from contact with cows. The view forward, across the fodder-gang, took in t'mew (mow = store of hay), with a hay-knife protruding from it. More hay had been stored on the baulks, above our head.

The cow being milked deftly collected the last few nutritious pellets in the big bucket and then created a noisy slurring sound as it licked the bucket clean. The cow in the next stall defacated sloppily and then sent a rivulet of urine coursing towards the drain. The farmer grunted as his cow swished its tail, which was covered with muck-buttons (pieces of dry dung). One of them had caught him across the cheek.

This was to be the last time I would see a small herd of Shorthorns being milked by hand. The Bordley man was devoted to his Shorthorns at a time when the Friesian was popular. He called the Friesian a "watter-can...it eats all afore it; aye, it has its head in t'barn and its rear-end ower t'midden." He had to stop milk production when his ancient buildings were inspected. They did not conform to modern standards of hygene.

For well over a century, the Shorthorn languished in the flower-decked fields or over-wintered in the many shippons or coo-houses, the name depending on whether you lived in Craven or the northern dales. A thrifty beast, the Shorthorn made few demands on the farm's resources, while providing good quality milk and beef. "A Shorthorn carried its age well. It was a good doer and a good milker and a good creamer. Aye, a Shorthorn would give milk without a lot of keep."

At the edge of human memory are the days when none of the milk left a hill farm as milk; it was skimmed, to be converted into butter or cheese (mainly butter) and what remained (the "blue" milk) was fed to the calves—or the hired man! The richness of Shorthorn milk was to be seen in the first flush following its delivery of a calf. Some of these "beastings" were made into a pudding, which resembled blancmange.

The Shorthorn was hardy, healthy and long-lived. "With its cock horns nicely turned up, it looked sprightly and young." There used to be a debate in the Dales about the form the horns should take—up or down. One farmer listened to the talk, then demolished the argument by remarking: "You don't get milk out of t'horns."

In the 1950s, changing methods of keeping cattle on a loose-housed, self-catering system led to the de-horning of stock. "Horns never troubled us in the old days; they were there and we never thought of taking 'em off." When BBC Television wanted some typical Dales cattle for the early instalments of the Herriot series, they went to Thomas Birkett's farm in Baldersdale, a tributary of Teesdale. He kept horned stock in the old-fashioned way.

At one time, before auction marts were opened, jobbers toured the Dales, buying up surplus stock. When Hawes mart was opened, it was still unhandy for the farmers of Upper Swaledale. Big Bill Alderson told me: "When I was a lad, I sometimes hed to lead a new-calved cow from our farm at Angram part way to the auction mart at Hawes. I went as far as Parting Liberties (on the Buttertubs Pass). Father, setting off later on horseback, met me and went on with the cow while I rode the horse home.

It was a two-day job for father. He sold his cow at the mart, stayed at Hawes overnight, and walked back next day." In the 1930s, a Swaledale man won first prize at Hawes, yet the successful cow brought him only £18. This animal had been walked to the market. "In those days, there wasn't cars flaying' aboot to disturb 'em."

Watering cattle in winter was an irksome task. The animals were released from the outbarns, which were built close to springs. "In a bad winter, there was plenty of snow for 'em to lick at. Snow blew in through cracks in the roof or around the doors."

Farmers in Upper Wensleydale turned out their milk cows on May 20, if the weather was settled. Young stock, or in-calf heifers, would have been released a week or so before. "The weather was t'boss, though an old chap who was a stickler for tradition let his milk cows out on May 20 even if they were bombarded with hailstones."

New-calved cows were kept near the farm and fed large quantities of oatmeal gruel, into which some linseed might be mixed to give the stock "a bit o' heat". A calf was so valuable in those straitened times that a Swaledale farmer sat up with a cow for a week before she dropped her calf. Great interest was shown in the calves. "What 'ev ye gitten?" a man would ask. "Oh I've gitten a great spand (red and white) bull cawf," the reply might be. White calves were called "wie" calves. A cow would be said to have dropped "a grand roan wie cawf—it's a bezzler."

It was customary to milk cattle out of doors, at the high pastures, in summer. The better land was growing grass which would be mown, wind and sun-dried into hay. The milking stool was placed in a tree or on a wall-top "where it wouldn't get wet and mucky". The cows were frisky at first and the dog was used to round them up. When they got into the milking routine, they knew their place. A handful of special feed in a bucket encouraged them to drop their milk. "I'd milk one, then turn to see an owd lass standing patiently, watching t'bucket, wi' slather running over her chin."

The milk was transported back to the farmhouse in a back-can. Or indeed, when times were impoverished, an attempt would be made to sell it direct, from cow to customer. In the 1930s, a Wensleydale farmer "got eight gallons o' milk, put it on my back, and selt it for 5d a gallon. I was better off than t'chaps in Coverdale, who were selling to Rowntrees at only 4½d a gallon."

In the 1930s, the milk demand by dairies increased. Motor vehicles with flat backs penetrated into Upper Swaledale, which had never been served by a railway. The lorries took loads of empty milk kits and collected those which had the morning milk in them, conveying the milk to a dairy at Leyburn.

With more milk needed, the Dales type of Shorthorn got a "smittlin'" of other dairy breeds, notably Ayrshire, and its great days were over...

Cow-Keepers of Liverpool

IT WAS A surprise when I asked Agnes Dawson, of Hellifield, where she was born. I had simply looked for confirmation that she had always lived in Hellifield, but Agnes (who before her marriage was one of the numerous Metcalfes) first saw the light of day in Liverpool. She rummaged in a drawer and brought out a photograph of her father, William, a little, spare chap, clad in his best setting-off suit as he drove a horse and milk float with Agnes and her sister Annie as passengers. A second print from the collection showed the family milkhouse. Writ large on the double doors were the words: W Metcalfe—Farmer and Cowkeeper.

I was told that Tommy Handley, of ITMA fame, on t'wireless, had come from Garsdale farming stock. His folk were among the many families who, when burgeoning Liverpool was cut off from the countryside by the Mersey and its sprawling new industries, took the country to the city and kept their little herds of Shorthorn cattle in unpromising circumstances to augment the local milk supply.

In the 1860s and 1870s, hundreds of families emigrated from the Dales, some (with lots of lads) heading for the collieries and steelworks of the north-east; yet more (having mainly lasses) settling in East Lancashire, where there were jobs in the textile mills) and an appreciable number developing mini-farming at Liverpool. This had its heyday in the years up to the 1914-18 war and, at the beginning of this century, resulted in several thousand cows were being kept within the city boundaries. It was ten-to-one there was a milkhouse at the end of the street. The citizens of Liverpool could get fresh milk whenever they fancied it.

A curious visitor to one of the new red-brick milkhouses—

and it must have aroused curiosity, with high buildings, high walls and high sliding door—would notice the basic elements. There was a dairy, of course, and a shippon where the cows stood and were milked; a stable, with hay stored in a loft; a shed into which the milk float might be backed, and a muck midden. All was scrupulously clean, the walls whitewashed, the ground swept regularly and given a covering of clean sawdust. Towards the end of the century, the Cowkeepers' Association came into being and an award was being made for the best-kept shippon and dairy.

The majority of cowkeepers hailed from the dale country of Yorkshire and Westmorland; they had left their native valleys to addle (earn) some brass and each of them dreamed of doing this well enough to allow them to buy a small farm in the dales and return to their roots. Meanwhile, in Liverpool, they worked "all hours God sent"—and took an hour off work on Sunday to go to church or chapel and thank God for his benevolence. The women had a twelve-hour-a-day stint in the dairy shop, where the items on sale included butter (some of it home-made) and hen eggs (invariably home-laid). The men (with womanly help) milked, mucked out, fed, scalded the dairy utensils and went on the rounds with the milk.

The cowkeepers of Liverpool maintained trading links with the Dales, buying many young in-calf cows. Cattle intended for Liverpool "must look as though they would give a canny drop o' milk, with good artificial feeding." When a cow finished its time—which meant that its milk yield had fallen below three gallons a day—it was taken to an abbatoir and its replacement was usually found at a Dales mart. The Liverpool type of Shorthorn, when released from the cowhouse, slipped and stumbled in an urban world where the only blades of grass were sprouting from cracks in the road. It was not unusual for a cow, sensing freedom, and agitated by the clamour around it, to run amok. Liverpudlians feared the rampaging Shorthorn.

Agnes Dawson, of Hellifield, hailed from a family of Metcalfes who lived in Garsdale, where her grandfather, John, his brother Thomas and son William (her father) were builders. Their skills were used on some of the viaducts when, in the 1870s, the Midland Railway Company pushed its new line through from Settle to Carlisle. Grandmother maintained home, family and nine or ten lodgers.

How William became a cowkeeper at Walton, then Fazackarley, is explained by the fact that when a cowkeeper named Holmes died, his stressful daughter travelled back to Garsdale for a holiday. The two met and married—in a Methodist chapel in Liverpool. The year was 1901. William settled down in a spot which was far in distance and spirit from the Dales. The Shorthorn cattle were exercised in a yard. The nearest curlews, reminders of home, were on the mudflats of the Mersey.

The family routine was bed-and-work. William's wife rose at 4-30 to hand-milk the cattle in the shippon so that when her husband clambered out of bed two hours later he could go on the milk round. Initially, he delivered milk to a few customers from cans he carried round the streets; then he bought a horse and float, followed by a motor cycle with a sidecar to hold two kits of milk. William was the first cowkeeper to invest in a car. The kits (usually known as churns) were accommodated on the running boards.

Young Agnes had a summertime job taking a horse-drawn lorry to Kirkdale Cemetery to collect a load of grass cuttings which supplemented the cows' daily ration. Some cowkeepers claimed grass from parks and grass verges. Other rations were fed in tubs adapted from treacle barrels, each barrel being sawn in two. The food provided at the twice-daily meal included exotic items like brewery waste, molasses, Indian linseed and pea meal, also grain and barley meal, with "thirds" and sometimes "sharps". Back in the Dales, the farmers needed every scrap of hay they could make. Their cousins in Liverpool bought hay from the South

Country and large quantities were also shipped in from Canada.

When father required additional cows, he approached two local dealers—Tommy Wolfenden and Sammy Lambert—who attended the marts at Skipton and Hellifield, sending the cattle to Liverpool by rail. The Metcalfes had their own Shorthorn bull which was kept in a shed made by father and daughter.

After twenty years of single-minded attention to his cowkeeping business, with some stressful days during the 1914-18 war, when Liverpool was a prime target for enemy bombs—William Metcalfe took a week-end off work so that he might re-visit Garsdale and buy Pry Hill, a farm of over a hundred acres which stood against The Street. To it he added Wood End, a holding of some seventy acres. When he left Fazackarley, he was a man of means who had forty-six cows—six of them in calf—and three horses.

William Metcalfe died in June, 1954. His wife had pre-deceased him by two years. The Liverpool and District Cowkeepers' Association was wound up in April, 1975.

The beauty of the dale country is more than skin-deep. The Great Scar Limestone is honeycombed with natural shafts (potholes) and galleries (caves). In the drawing above, potholers are shown in Alum Pot, near Selside. The potholer (right) is typical in his dress of the explorers of the immediate post-war years.

One Way Down Gaping Gill

A BOSUN'S chair descent into the main chamber of Gaping Gill, our largest natural cavern, is one of the more unusual pastimes for a Bank Holiday Weekend. The chair is attached by wire rope to a winch. Once clear of the mossy walls of the upper shaft, the passenger finds him/herself in smooth and rapid descent. The sensation is similar to that of a spider dangling from the dome of St Paul's. Twenty seconds (and 340 ft) later, the descent ends with a gentle landing on shingle.

Each spring, the Bradford Pothole Club holds a Meet at GG, going to enormous trouble to erect a gantry, winch and bosun's chair. Normally, a beck leaps from the rim of the pothole and falls over twice the height of Niagara. When Meets are held, the beck is dammed and water is diverted into another part of the system. Last year, when the Craven Club had their meet at Gaping Gill, and similar equipment was erected, there must have been a subtle change in the natural plumbing of the mountain. No water leaked from the dam but underground I passed briefly through Yorkshire's biggest shower-bath.

Gaping Gill, which is usually approached from Clapham, via the Woods and Trow Gill, is the monarch of Yorkshire potholes. Several ways into the system are known but the most impressive is down the main shaft, into gloomy wetness and what Reginald Farrer (the plant collector, born at Clapham) described as "a dim and awful world".

Journalists have stood in awe of GG and reserved for it some of their most telling phrases. The chamber is truly vast. Photographers have tried (with moderate success) to capture a good image of our largest natural chamber. The most recent was that of the chief photographer of a Yorkshire newspaper who, with the backing of "computer wizardry", sought to superimpose an image of the main tower of York Minster (photographed in colour) with GG (taken in monochrome but given a sepia tint to harmonise with the Minster's stone). Readers were told that both negatives were scanned electronically into a computer and electronically "married" to create the double-image effect.

Eli Simpson, who was caving in the 1930s, responded to the challenge of GG, setting up his plate camera and then distributing across the vast floor crumpled pieces of newspaper holding flash-powder. He opened the lens of the camera and systematically set off the flash-powder, with awesome results. It was not so much the light that impressed as the dense smoke which followed. Simpson remarked: "The worst job was finding the camera." It was Simpson who, at the time of the Coronation, took a photograph of cavers toasting the King's health in the depths of GG. (The picture had been taken several days before).

The centenary of the first successful descent of GG falls in 1995. A Yorkshireman, Edward Calvert, hoped to set foot there in 1894 but dates were fixed and postponed. It was a French speleologist, E A Martel, who accomplished the feat—and returned to tell the tale. Martel was hyperactive. In 1895, the year of his triumph in the bowels of Ingleborough, he wrote a book about the Alps, read a paper on speology at a geological congress in London, visited caverns in Derbyshire and subterranean rivers in Ireland. He also surveyed a new Irish cave.

Martel's only experienced back-up was provided by his wife, who was on telephone duty. The agile Frenchman left a brief account of his descent with Harry Harrison, guide to Ingleborough Cave, and wrote in the visiting book at the New Inn, Clapham: "On Thursday, August 1, I went down Gaper Gill hole, etc." He later recalled in the *Journal* of the Alpine Club: "There were no stalactites or sparkling diamonds of carbonate of lime to be seen (the cave is too frequently flooded with water for that). It is an immense cathedral unsupported by a single pillar...One vast hall, 500 ft long, 80 to 100 ft high, 66 to 125 ft broad..."

Among the hundred people who watched Martel descend was a young lad I knew in his later years as W K Mattinson, of Austwick. It was with members of the Austwick Field Club, including Mattinson's daughter and grandson, that I made my own first descent of GG. Who was the first woman to reach the vast floor of the main chamber? Many years ago, after talking to the Wharfedale Naturalists at Ilkley, I was approached by an old lady—Miss Mary Booth, of Ben Rhydding—who claimed this distinction. (She had also crossed the Gobi Desert by camel and, on another hazardous expedition, was captured by Chinese pirates).

Dr S A Craven, who grew up in Ilkley, spent much time in the Limestone Country and has lived for many years in South Africa, wrote to me recently that Miss Booth was one of four ladies who made the second female descent, in June, 1906. The first lady to descend the pothole was Miss L E May Johnson, of Bradwell, Derbyshire, who was attending a Meet of the short-lived and little-known Leeds Ramblers' Club in 1904.

My favourite story concerning a potholer dates back almost fifty years ago, when I was sitting in a Pennine bus at Settle. A young lad clambered board. He carried a section of rope ladder. An old lady asked him: "Are you one of these pothoiler chaps?" He nodded. We all chuckled when she sighed and remarked: "Eh, lad—doesn't ta think tha'll spend enuff time below t'grund wi'out going there now?"

Springtime Into Summer

Our road for the greater part lay over wild uncultivated moors feeding a few Scots and black faced sheep, amongst high and bleak hills with the river Ure...winding and foaming in the bottom.

Charles Fothergill (1805).

To me it is in a misty atmosphere that Simon's Seat is at its best. I like it so because it is easy to catch it in this mood. Dull misty days predominate in the Yorkshire dales, and I prefer common things to exceptional ones.

Chiang Yee, a Chinese visitor to Wharfedale (1941).

The Dalesman may live for a life-time under the same roof, and yet never weary of a land whose face is for ever changing, for ever showing some new wonder at the bidding of wind and sun and rain.

Halliwell Sutcliffe, The Striding Dales (1929).

A Dales Clipping-Time

FOUNTAINS FELL, one of the great sheep ridges of the Craven district, is named after Fountains Abbey, which stood by the Skell near Ripon and had a million acres of grazing land on the Pennines. Each summer, shepherds gathered the crag-sheep and drove them to the grange at Kilnsey, where they were dipped in water to remove the moorland grit and help the new wool to rise.

A fortnight or so later came clipping time. The hand-shears used were in appearance not unlike those held by the fathers of our present Dales farmers. The bundles of wool were transported in ox-drawn wains across the moors to Fountains, here to be stored in the cellarium, awaiting the arrival of dealers from the Continent. Yorkshire wool was then part of a lively export trade with mainland Europe.

Clipping-time is nigh. Despite the cool wind, many tups have already been shorn and, by the time of the autumn sales at Hawes or Kirkby Stephen, will have grown enough new wool to look appealing to buyers. Next to be clipped are the hoggs (last year's lambs), followed by the ewes, the bulk of the flock.

A Keasden farmer told me the story of a June wash-day when the farmers awoke to find that their collies had cleared off. "My dad said we might find 'em up at t'wash-dub. So we all traipsed (walked) up there. Sure enough, t'dogs had rounded up them sheep." At this stage of the narrative, it was possible that the story might be true. Then (untypically) this farmer entered the realms of fantasy. "One dog was chucking sheep into t'watter. Another dog was weshin' 'em. Someone asked my dad what our dog was doing and he said: 'Goin' round wi' t'bottle'."

Washing also released into the water traces of the salve applied to the skins of hill sheep in the previous November. Salve was made by heating in a cauldron some Stockholm tar, rancid butter and "a bit o' milk to take t'sting oot on it." An old farmer from Littondale told me his brother was married in "salving time" and his hands were jet black.

I enjoy looking at photographs of Dales life as it was, and especially those pictures showing the boon-clip at a farm where the sheep numbered a thousand or more. A small army of neighbours, friends and family—none of them expecting to be paid—dealt with the flock and had enough energy left, following a gargantuan meal, to dance half the night away. Next day, the helpers moved to another farm.

At a place like Lamb Hill, just over Burnmoor from Clapham, there were over eighty workers, half of them holding shears. Others renewed the marks on shorn sheep and folded and stored the fleeces. Women, with long white pinafores over their dresses ensured that none of the workers was short of drink or food (in that order). There followed the customary savoury meal. Dancing in the big barn was to the music of fiddle and concertina.

Today, the snip of hand-shears is rarely heard, except where retired farmers, having mown their lawns, use shears to trim the edges! It was a treat in the old days to visit upper Swaledale, for example, and see clipping taking place in a croft beside the road. The clippers sat on stocks. They wore the typical Dales farmer's clothing—fustian breeches, held up with galluses (braces) thick (and therefore durable) shirt and cap with a neb "to keep t'sun out of mi eyes." Sheep which began to cast their wool naturally in spring, when they were suckling lambs, were said by a Dales farmer to have "clipped thersens".

The successors of these men put sheep-clipping out to contract. A clipping gang consists of two or three men who have the ability to clip between 200 and 400 sheep in a single day. The old stool or stock on which the Dales farmer sat, beside the sheep he was clipping, has become a museum piece. A farmer would quell a restless sheep by fastening some band round the hind legs. Who'd be a sheep?

Modern team-clippers use the Bowen technique, as devised by Sir Godfrey Bowen. A sheep being shorn is gripped between the legs of the shearer at the beginning and end of the operation. "We just work the sheep round," I was told. When the sheep has been divested of its wool, in a minute or two, the clipper opens his legs and the sheep scurries away, while work begins on the next animal.

Hoggs are lively sheep, being about eighteen months old. "It's hard work," said a young man holding some power-shears. "Hoggs are thick wi' wool which has bits of peat and grit in it. Because they've not been clipped afore, they don't know how to behave. They can be awkward." Clippers from New Zealand "curse and swear" when they see a Dales sheep, with its formidable horns. "I was used to clipping hornless sheep. I didn't fancy holding a horned animal between my legs," said one of them.

Major Horner, who presided over the *White Lion*, Cray, at the head of Wharfedale, showed me a framed letter he had received from a Bradford wool merchant in 1930. It related to a bid to break the world record for wool "from the sheep's back to the finished suit." (Incidentally, Major was a Christian name and not a military title).

The wool merchant, J H Denby, who had farming interests in Upper Wharfedale, arranged for four Dales farmers to stay at his Bradford home on the previous night. Six sheep, all Swaledales, were divested of their wool in the mill. The whole process through to the making of the suit lasted three hours, twenty and a half minutes. With the framed letter was a small piece of record-breaking cloth.

I asked a Wharfedale farmer about the current price of wool. He shook his head and replied: "It's bin a lot better, lad." He reflected for a few moments, then added: "By t'time I've paid t'contract clippers between 40p and 50p a sheep, I might just have well have left t'wool on t'sheep's back."

Dalesmen Who Took the "Road to the Isles"

MANY A Dales farmer has combined business with pleasure while holidaymaking at Oban, on the Argyll coast of Scotland. A ripple of interest has just passed along the Pennines with the news of the opening of Oban Livestock Centre, a £750,000 successor to the old mart. The young man who today drives a cattle wagon from the Dales to Oban, to buy beef cattle, is the successor of the old-time drover, who moved stock over vast distances on the hoof.

When the Settle-Carlisle railway was opened for goods traffic in 1895, a Dales cattle dealer was able to catch the Scots express to attend an autumn sale. He arranged for the stock he bought to be consigned to Garsdale or Ribblehead or Bell Busk by train. Cattle reared on the lean grazings of the "blue islands" soon filled out their frames while grazing hock-deep in the rich grass of Craven.

A man lately retired from farming in North Ribblesdale told me of a recent Scottish holiday. He and his wife went to the Hebrides, returning via Mull and Oban. He then drove southwards from the town to Seil Island, not to cross "the only bridge over the Atlantic" but (en route) to see how t'new auction mart was shaping up!

I asked Edith Carr if she had been to Oban. She most certainly had, as a young lass, in the company of her cattle-buying uncles, who farmed at Hanlith Hall, in Malhamdale. They stayed for two days at the *Argyll Hotel* and bought about 30 island cattle, paying about £15 a beast.

Two main types of cattle were on offer—the "gingery, long-horned variety" and a dark, polled type, akin to the

Aberdeen Angus. "There were lots of drovers available to help us put them in the cattle wagons at Oban railway station. It was a different matter when they were let out at Bell Busk, the nearest station to Malhamdale."

Mr Bateson, the stationmaster, a former policeman "who was used to giving directions", tried to control the unruly Scotch cattle. "They were wild. No dog could turn them. They set off at a gallop and everyone who turned up to help had to keep up the same pace, hoping to block all the gateways. It was a right tussle." In spring, when the cattle were sold, they were much more docile and had filled out their frames with good eating.

The Dales connection with cattle dealing in the Highlands and Islands goes back two hundred years. In 1745, when the Highlands were aflame with Jacobean fervour, a grazier named John Birtwhistle of Skipton travelled north to buy cattle. The Highlanders distinguished between politics and business. No one molested Mr Birtwhistle.

Back home, he rented the Great Close, a 730-acre tract of grassland near Malham Tarn, as a reception area for the droves of vulgar (black) cattle which had been driven vast distances. Some had originally swum the kyles from their native islands to the mainland. An old chap in the Northern Dales used to talk about his forebears buying "kyloes". Our information about Birtwhistle and his cattle comes from the writings (1834) of Thomas Hurtley, the Malham schoolmaster, who I suspect was "a bit of a romancer". Were there really 5,000 of Birtwhistle's cattle refreshing themselves on Great Close at one time?

The Hon John Byng, in describing a journey on horseback he made in 1792 mentioned arriving at Grierstones (Gearstones) near Ribblehead, which was "the seat of misery, in a desert." Unluckily for Byng, he had to share accommodation with those attending "the Scotch fair held upon the heath"—a sight which "added to the horror of this curious scenery."

The heyday of cattle-droving was in the eighteenth and nineteenth centuries, Vast numbers of cattle from Scotland (and from Wales and Ireland also) were needed to meet the demand for fresh beef from families in the burgeoning industrial towns of northern England and the Midlands.

Mrs Mason, of Gayle, remembers when as a child she accompanied her father to Alston to pay off a Scotch drover. The cattle he delivered were driven on the last stretch of the journey with an English attendant. Her father was a notable cattle dealer. When she was a girl, she slipped a warm coat over her nightgown to drive a horse and trap to Garsdale station where—he being such a good customer—the Scotch express would be stopped specially for him. It was autumn and the weather was chill. On her return, she reined in the horse at Appersett, near Hawes, where a kindly old lady who was standing in the road said: "Ee—you'll be starved (chilled) through. Come and have a cup of tea."

When, a few years ago, Border Television decided to make a film about cattle-droving, I met the crew (and their wayward cattle) at Kilnsey in Wharfedale and followed them across Mastiles Lane to the traditional area near Great Close, where the night was to be spent. Eric Robson and Clem Shaw, as co-producers, had originally planned the Yorkshire stretch across Yew Cogar and adjacent scars, with the permission of local landowners. When they walked the route, it was fine for four-fifths of the way. Then they came across a wall and stile. The cattle had been trained pretty well but "we reckoned that getting some Highland cattle and up to thirty Galloways over a stile was pushing our luck a bit."

When the television company outlined its scheme, a vet advised that modern cattle would not have the staying power of the old-timers; they would have to be moved from area to area by cattle wagon. The Cumbrian driver, who was used to hills, shuddered at the sight of the zig-zagging road on the brow beyond Darnbrook Farm.

For once, the cattle had an easy crossing.

Life with the Flopwing

THE YOUNG lapwings which hatched at the rough edges of the Dales as balls of wool on stilt-like wings soon cast off the down of infancy. The lapwing is well-named. A flock crosses the grey sky with a distinctive twinkling effect, produced by the slow movement of tufty wings and the dark and light contrasts of the plumage.

From the bird's contact call, pee-wit, comes another familiar name. The dalesman knows this bird as "tewit" and the moist places where it nests as "tewit-grund". Cool, dry weather has not suited the tewits this year. With much of the ground hard and cracked, food was scarcer than usual.

Rudyard Kipling, who had family associations with Skipton, wrote a story featuring his famous Soldiers Three, on duty in India. One of the men recalled days spent on Greenhow Hill, in his native Yorkshire. He was particularly nostalgic as he thought of the tewits, circling and calling in the thin air. Richard Kearton, son of a Swaledale gamekeeper and one of the pioneers of bird photography, was familiar with this noisy bird, which he took pleasure in photographing.

My fondness for the tewit, whose reedy voice catches the spirit of the Dales, as does none other but the bubbling call of the curlew, dates back to the time I was a member of the 5th Skipton Boy Scout Troop. We periodically camped at Potter Ghyll, a gash in the side of Rombald's Moor. To reach the ghyll we had to haul our trek-cart across a big pasture—one tufty with sieves (rushes) and holding wet spots where in spring the lapwings wheeled and wailed.

Sometimes a bird showed its annoyance by making a buzzing sound through agitated movements of its bottle-green wings. Cock birds have especially long head-crests. Also conspicuous is the russet brown of the undertail coverts.

Hearing tewits calling and flying with throbbing wings during this current springtime brought into mind Stevenson's famous lines about "wine red moors" and "hills of home", where you might "hear about the graves of the martyrs the pee-wees crying." Luvly.

I watched a tewit displaying on a rough pasture near the source of the Ribble; another was showing-off by Sulber Nick, on a popular approach to Ingleborough. And while using the unfenced road which extends like a grey ribbon across the moors from Upper Swaledale to Nateby, in Mallerstang, I had to stop the car to allow some lapwing chicks, attended by fretful adults, to clear the tarmac.

Birds return to the nesting grounds as early as mid-February. I see birds in a pair flying slowly, close together. In early spring, too, there is a combination of vocal and wing music. A cock bird rises, gives an exuberant *pwee-eee-weep* and flicks over, to make a rapid descent. The wings, which always remind me of the ears of a cocker spaniel, produce a deep and vibrant sound, rather like *wup wup wup*.

There's another lively outburst before the bird pulls out of its dive. You might think it was intent on dashing itself against the ground. Instead, it makes a sedate landing—on two feet! A friend, seeing this display, christened the bird "flopwing".

The springtime display at a big sheep farm back o' Penyghent was captured, many years ago, by a BBC film crew. They were "shooting" *Pastures in High Places*, with Stanley Williamson as the producer. He had arranged to follow the fortunes of John Coates and his family, of Rainscar, throughout the year.

The flight sequence was followed by a close-up of the nest, with its clutch of four large, pear-shaped eggs, which are brown or stone-coloured, with dark blotches, and recline in a shallow scrape. In the pre-slurry days, when farmyard manure was spread in lumps, pieces of straw—thick and bleached—were used by some tewits and readily marked the position of the nest.

The romantic picture of the tewit is of a bird nesting in an isolated area, such as a moor-edge, with the crumbling remains of a hill farm in the background and land, hard won from the moor by generations of dalesfolk, reverting (through neglect) to rush and bracken. In fact, you will find lapwings in fields beside busy roads, the cock bird extending its territorial flights over the fast-moving traffic. Motorists see birds feeding in the distinctive lapwing way, with unbent legs. It looks as if the body is tilting on a pivot.

An anxious adult bird soon signals to its young, which flop and "freeze" to escape detection. I found one tewit chick resting in the print of a horse's hoof.

"Blackbird" in a Dinner Jacket

FROM THE moorland track between Swinnergill and Gunnerside Gill, in Upper Swaledale, I viewed a trio of hills with grand-sounding names—Great Shunner Fell, Mallerstang Edge and Nine Standards Rigg.

I had parked my car just off the road near the home of Matthew Cherry, who years ago gave me a conducted tour of the Swaledale mining area. I was on familiar ground, between two gills desecrated by t'Owd Man, the collective name for generations of miners.

Around the ruined buildings, the ground was spangled by the starry white of spring sandwort, a plant tolerant of lead. The well-masoned entrances to underground systems were now festooned with ferns. On the high pastures, yellow mountain pansies fluttered in the merest breeze. Some had splashes of purple on their upper leaves. A passing tourist called them "Mickey Mouse pansies."

I ventured into Swinnergill Kirk, a cave at the head of the gorge which is said to have been the meeting place for Nonconformists at a time of religious intolerance. Four-inch-long black slugs luxuriated in a mini-jungle kept moist by spray from a fan-shaped waterfall.

My old friend Bill Robson would have diagnosed this as "ring ouzel country", referring to our white-bibbed "mountain blackbird". The cool notes of a cock bird are given a special quality when uttered in the echo-chamber of a Pennine gill. I was to hear ouzel voices throughout the day.

My first sighting of ring ouzels was at the edge of a gritstone moor. The birds were blackbirdish in shape and in their quick, nervous movements. But the cock bird had a white gorget set against the dark plumage. I noticed even then that it looked to be a dusty plumage, as though the bird had been sprinkled with flour. What I was seeing was the effect of white edging to the feathers. The hen ouzel is a duller version of her mate.

My regard for the Pennine ring ouzel developed in the company of Bill Robson, who was a farmer for six days of the week and, on the seventh, indulged his love of natural history. Each expedition began with hot coffee and scones in his big farm kitchen. From March to September we often saw ring ouzels in gills which Bill had explored since boyhood. I had a fanciful idea the cock birds had to report to him when they arrived at the end of March from wintering areas beside the Mediterranean. (Some Pennine birds winter on the Atlas Mountains of North Africa).

By the end of the month, birds which had returned to the Dales to nest were vocal, proclaiming their territories. Soon they were joined by the females. Nesting began. In a limestone area, one pair nested on a ledge within a pothole—a cosy situation, away from the bitter winds. Another pair nested on an aluminium girder in the fuselage of a wrecked Stirling bomber which crashed on to Mickle Fell during the 1939-45 war. (Until 1974, when the Government played fast and loose with the boundaries, Mickle Fell was the highest hill in Yorkshire).

On a walk across a tract of commonland, I entered a derelict building to find a pair of blackbirds nesting in a ground floor room and a pair of ring ouzels (the "mountain" version) with a nest in one of the bedrooms. Stan Lythe, of Grassington, built up a fine collection of photographs of ring ouzels nesting in one of the gills edging Grassington Moor. Stan and his wife Kath photographed a pair at a bracken-screened nest on a bank. When the chicks fledged, they were fed under cover of the bracken, which was now growing fast.

Towards the end of June, Stan and Kath found a further two nests higher up the gill. These had been set on rock ledges near some lead-mine spoilheaps. Ring ouzels may even attempt to nest a third time, prolonging the nesting season well into July.

Ian Appleyard, the most dedicated of ouzel-watchers, became aware of the ouzel's distinctive flight—"more dashing and direct than the blackbird's; its wings appear to flicker, particularly as it travels away from one." He notes that in August and September, family groups are to be seen roaming the uplands for berries and other food.

The Railway in the Clouds

SETTLE-CARLITIS is an incurable disease. The sufferers do not wish to be cured. I was first afflicted over forty years ago when I wandered into the waiting room at Ribblehead, saw a harmonium—"an ill wind which nobody blows any good"—inquired about why it was there, and became fascinated by tales told of those who made and sustained this railway in the clouds.

My godfather, one of the drivers who thrashed the old steam locomotives up the Long Drag from Settle, fed me with good stories, such as that of the old lady living near the line who ensured she had a supply of free coal by placing a row of bottles on her garden wall, confident that no fireman could resist lobbing some coal at them.

I coined the term Settle-Carlitis in 1962. The symptons are a fevered brow, palpitations and an urge to watch the local trains, preferably steam-hauled but, if needs must, even the unspectacular Pacer. There might be a spell of a few weeks when Settle-Carlitis lies dormant; then, with a whiff of train-smoke, the toot of a whistle or yet another spiffing yarn about the line, S-C returns.

I was just recovering from a major attack of Settle-Carlitis induced by seeing Julia Darling's dramatic reconstruction of shany town life in *Head of Steel* when Sophie Weston, who is in charge of music at Catteral Hall, the preparatory school of Giggleswick, arrived at my home with an offer I just could not refuse—to narrate *Running on Rails,* a new musical production about the building of the Settle-Carlisle.

Sophie produced the score and libretto in printed form. The pages were adorned with Betty Harrington's famous reconstructions of shanty life at Ribblehead. On the cover was the number 72, endlessly repeated. As everyone should know, the railway is 72 miles long. Not long before, in a conversation about cricket, a Settle man had related that Constantine, the West Indian cricketer who was also a professional with a club in East Lancashire, was battling on the Settle ground when he drove a ball all those 72 miles (it fell into the wagon of a passing goods train and was taken out at Carlisle).

Now I heard that Catteral Hall, which was established sixty years ago, had a cantata specially written by Jan Holdstock of Leeds, whose music has been a feature of events at the school. The latest composition would evoke "navvy time", when 2,000 men and their families lived in the hutments of Ribblehead and Mr Tiplady, an evangelist appointed by the Bradford City Mission, opened a chapel in a wooden hut.

The world premiere of *Running on Rails,* at the Northern Preparatory Schools' Music Day, would be given by a choir of 120, representing Aysgarth, Malsis Hall, Ripon Cathedral Choir School and Catteral Hall. Simon Lindley, organist and choirmaster at Leeds Parish Church, would lead the final rehearsal and conduct the first performance.

Having given a spirited rendering of *Oliver!* Catteral Hall turned its attention to *Running On Rails.* In reality, these were steel rails, laid by Midland men when the railway was built between the years 1869 and 1875. The course of the Settle-Carlisle is little more than a mile from the school.

On the day appointed for music-making, Jan Holdstock, who had travelled in from Leeds, was given the affable reception accorded to an old friend. When her musical play *Christopher Columbus* was performed in 1992, the school asked her to write a special piece for them. Here was the result—five songs linked by Pat Belford's narration.

The music having been rehearsed by choristers at four different schools, a rehearsal of the group was vital for what the programme for the day described as "this somewhat (necessarily) ad hoc first performance." A few hours before the premiere, Simon Lindley introduced himself to the large choir. He then began to tease from them a performance which improved and increased in volume by the minute.

With piano and drums providing an accompaniment, and Simon urging the young choristers to ever-greater efforts, the songs lived. *Seventy Two Miles of Rail* ended with an appropriate shhhh (as the locomotive came to a halt at Carlisle). *Pennine Weather Song* provided a contrast between languid summer days and a winter when the snow "freezes and it flurries". I recalled to myself winter days, with a fringe of icicles on the water tank at Blea Moor. A brazier burned beside the water-crane and locomotives fitted with snowploughs were lumbering towards Dent Cutting.

As narrator, my greatest moment came in the run-up to a calyso referring to "a wonderful new invention, costing £200 per ton" which "was transported by road to the hills for blasting the rock...its name was Dynamite!" A second later, Simon and the children began *Dynamite Calypso* with an appropriate explosion of sound.

During the singing, I glanced to where the composer was sitting. Her feet were tapping. Nearby, Sophie Weston was smiling. The choir itself was following Simon Lindley's injunction to look happy. A cantata called *Running on Rails* had (musically) stayed on the track.

Shy Man Who Opened Up
The Fells

BEFORE LONG, I must go looking for bilberries and some fresh sheep droppings. Each year, I intend to photograph them, side by side, for a Dales slide show in which I recall that great fellgoer, Alfred Wainwright, who was as much a Dalesman as a Lakelander. Wainwright wrote that anyone who takes up fell-walking should, as a matter of urgency, be able to tell the difference between bilberries and sheep droppings. (Bilberries are inclined to taste the sweetest!).

I knew Wainwright well. We first met just before he published the first of his famous pictorial guides to the Lake District and before he devised guides to the Pennine Way and Limestone Yorkshire. I had hoped to interview him. He agreed to meet me. He looked affable, whenever he emerged from clouds of pipe-smoke. But he adroitly dodged my questions. Half an hour later, I concluded he did not want to be interviewed. Not for many years did AW, overcoming his natural shyness and reserve, become a media celebrity. We met, now and again, or he typed me a brief letter, signing it (in green ink) first A Wainwright and then simply AW, a mark of friendship.

Wainwright was quirky, crotchety, taciturn—and lovable. He preferred to walk alone, in the spirit of Matthew Arnold, who wrote of "the cheerful silence of the fells". If AW saw an approaching party of schoolchildren or ramblers, he tried to avoid them or he slipped out of sight behind a boulder. In contrast with the modern rambler, with his/her fashionable, multi-coloured, all-weather garb, Wainwright donned or-dinary clothes, a well-worn raincoat with pockets (large enough to hold his pipe and tobacco pouch) and a cloth cap, as though testifying to his North Country milltown ancestry. His boots were just ordinary boots, with nails for extra grip.

He used public transport extensively, never carried a compass, and not only used the Ordnance Survey as the basis of his maps but periodically wrote to them suggesting modifications. Three of his guides—for the Pennine Way, Coast to Coast and Limestone Country—include notes and pictures of the Dales, which he first got to know in 1938 when, still living in Blackburn, he travelled to Settle and trudged northwards on the Pennines to Hadrian's Wall.

Wainwright wrote up his experiences as *A Pennine Journey*, which was to be published (its text virtually unchanged) almost fifty years later. He was already displaying style and originality in his writing. One day in North Ribblesdale "my shadow was my sole companion". The "somewhat shabby" church at Horton reared its old head above the cottage roofs, "signifying that it has lost none of its pride." At Hubberholme, in Upper Wharfedale, he stayed overnight in the home of Mrs Falshaw. She had first scrutinished him as though he were "a visitor from another planet".

AW glorified in the high fells—the region where, as Halliwell Sutcliffe once wrote, "lean lands rake the sky". When he was preparing his pictorial guides, he devised one page each evening, writing in miniscule but immaculate script and filling in the gaps with his fine penmanship, which took the form of maps or drawings. Twice a week he took time off to watch *Coronation Street* on television. It reminded him of his Lancashire milltown upbringing. As a fish-and-chip fanatic, a partiality which developed in his milltown days, AW was delighted when he was taken by a printer to Harry Ramsden's. Sue Lawley, interviewing him for the radio programme *Desert Island Discs* heard him ask, plaintively: "Will there be a chip shop on the island?"

Having just completed the western section of Wainwright's

Coast to Coast—a walk of 95 miles, with a total of 12,000 feet of climbing—I frequently think of Wainwright who pioneered a route which is now followed by about 6,000 people a year. Wainwright's guide books are somewhat out-of-date and in process of being revised. It amused me at one port of call on the Coast to Coast to hear of the two ladies who set off from St Bee's, not knowing of the guide book and trying to find their way using the coffee-table version, with its large print and colour pictures. They thought that Dent, the first major hill, was a town and looked forward to calling at the bank for more cash.

My walk ended at Keld, head of Swaledale (where I will begin the eastern section next spring). On that last golden day, I made the steady climb from Kirkby Stephen to Nine Standards Rigg, followed by a moorland crossing to Whitsun Dale and Raven Seat. A couple from Worthing who were walking from east to west—they had left their car at St Bee's and paid £120 for a taxi trip to Robin Hood's Bay—displayed their multi-blistered feet but still spoke appreciatively of AW and his footpath creation.

Though he eventually agreed to newspaper and television requests to be interviewed, he did not overcome his diffidence in the presence of others. He died in January, 1991. His last upland walk was on a day when it never stopped raining. Said AW, wet and dispirited: "The mountains wept for me." His ashes were scattered beside Innominate Tarn on Haystacks.

Return of the Roe and the Red Deer

A KEEN gardener at Langcliffe, in North Ribblesdale, has been having his favourite rose bushes pruned by a roebuck which has been making nocturnal visits to the garden. A lady living at Willow Wood, a mile up the dale, reported seeing "a few small deer" among the trees near Craven Quarry. A roe buck was seen clattering across a quarry further up the dale. A year or so ago, roe deer were reported to be in woodland behind Malham Tarn House, at an elevation of over 1,000 feet.

From many parts of the Dales come reports that our smallest native deer is in residence. The spread of roe deer has been county-wide. At Cliffe Castle, Keighley, where many natural history records are kept, I was told of the roe which startled a Bradford milkman when it cantered by—in Manningham Lane! The all-conquering roe deer has made a two-pronged invasion of the Dales. Footloose young animals were in the vanguard. Roe from Southern Lakeland, as insubstantial as shadows in the gloaming, crossed Lunesdale and traversed the Wenning Valley. Some extended the range into Limestone Craven and others crossed the high ridge into Bowland.

Meanwhile, the surplus roe of the huge Border Forests spread to the lower dales and moved "upbank". Many years have elapsed since I flushed a testy roebuck in one of the high hills of Swaledale. I heard a gruff bark, almost like a smoker's cough. The animal which broke cover stood among some thorns, the dappling effect of light and shade breaking up the chunky form and the foxy-red of its coat. A roebuck has a pair of small horns. I noticed the moustachial stripe and, before

LETTERS FROM THE DALES

it bounced away, the white rump disc, shaped like a kidney.

The roe deer is a true native, being well established before the "land bridge" connecting what is now Britain to the Continent was washed away, leaving us with an island status. Roe benefited from the almost continuous forest conditions and then were robbed of cover by the spread of farming and ultimately of towns. Roe were also prized as creatures of the chase. Early this century, one or two roe may have survived in woodland where the Dales run into the Plain. I recall meeting an old warrior on Solway Moss, where the breed hung on and eventually re-colonised northern Lakeland. The southern part of the district was in due course over-run by Austrian-type roe released on an estate west of Windermere.

The re-colonisation of the Dales has been phenomenal, considering the size of the roe. It is classified as "small" but even so would stand out prominently but for its cryptic colouration and its ability to remain motionless when danger threatens. The success of the breed is partly due to its disposition to be a loner. Roe are not herding animals. In high summer, a doe can slip into an area and drop a pair of kids without being noticed. Shortly afterwards, the doe permits herself to be mated again. A process of "delayed implantation" ensures that the kids will be born in summer, a time of maximum cover, when there is a bounty of good food.

The red deer, largest of our native mammals, arrived in the Dales some six thousand years ago to share the fellside grazings with sheep. The sheep eventually triumphed, through sheer force of numbers, and by the end of the eighteenth century the last pockets of wild red deer were gone. Eric Foster, who farmed at Little Newton, east of Hellifield Station, imported some red deer from a south country park. They arrived, courtesy of British Rail and, once released, spread out, to be rounded up by Eric who mountained a horse, Western style.

Eventually, the deer were "heafed", being content to remain in certain fields. From their youngest days, Eric had discouraged them from leaping walls. One evening, as I chatted with him, he excused himself and said: "I'll just go across to the deer and ask them if they'd like a change of field." He actually whispered into the ear of one of them. The field gate was left open and soon they were on the move to new land. A visit to Eric ended with what he called a prayer meeting. He summoned his three dogs. They clambered on to the protruding stones of a stile and, at a command, they bowed their heads until a simple prayer had been spoken.

In summer, Eric's stags were inclined to lie out on Long Preston Moor. They re-joined the hinds for the autumn rut. One old stag, which must have been usurped as leader by a younger animal, left the farm and became "The Muckle Stag of Giggleswick". A postman, on his rounds in the west of the parish, reported "a gurt big deer". Not everyone believed him. I visited the farm, trudged for half an hour across the fields, then descended into a gill, thinking the postman had been mistaken.

Here was the Muckle Stag, to use a Scottish word for "great". We stared at each other from a range of fifty yards. The stag's antlers were "going back". He must have been over six years old. One ear had been torn. The coat was dark because he had been wallowing. I mentioned the stag to a farmer friend, Arthur Hodgson, who on his next visit to Settle market made a detour to call at the farm. Arthur "shot" the stag, using a camera. The beast was pictured on the skyline, with the profile of Ingleborough showing up grandly beyond.

In High Summer

WILD ROSE

The blue geranium, known as meadow cranesbill, lines the roadside verges where it mixes with the somewhat paler, tall, blue spikes of giant bellflower. The mountain pansy is widely scattered on pastures and grassland.

A David Leather (1992).

In the most lofty and inhospitable places, the growing season lasts for a mere one-third of the year, but down in the valleys...is almost everywhere longer than 200 days.

Richard Muir, The Dales of Yorkshire (1991).

Through the Dales there is visual harmony both in the intimate scene or in the wide view from a windy hill.

Geoffrey N Wright (1985).

Old Ghosts in the Farmstead Ruins

ON THE the marginal lands, farmsteads which have been vacated for years lie in an advanced state of ruin. They remind us of the old frontier between rough pastures and the moor. The owner of one upper Dales estate—a water authority—arranged for half a dozen farmhouses to be blown up. The walls of one house fell neatly inwards and the roof dropped on top. An undamaged chimney pot is now used as a plant pot by a local gardener. It was an eerie sensation for me to crawl between ranks of sitka spruce and see the remains of another farm across a mossy glade. Ferns and mosses lagged a flight of steps in a wall. An old privvy (outside closet) was cocooned by fine mosses.

Such little groups of buildings thrived with what I think of as the Dales "fellside culture". A century and more ago, big families, fiercely self-reliant, occupied these small farms and managed to keep them viable despite the pathetically small resources. They had maybe a dozen cows, plus some sheep on the moor, from which also came the domestic fuel (peat). These uplanders were realistic, taciturn and thrifty. They helped one another.

A schoolgirl, walking the three miles from home to her lessons, saw a group of sad people standing at a farm which was one of the smallest, with only two acres of meadow. She later heard her parents discuss what had happened. The only horse they owned had dropped dead. Her father subsequently gave the small lass sixpence and said: "Get me the cheapest notebook they sell at the village shop...and don't spend anything on sweets."

Years later, while going through her dead father's posses-
sions, she came across the little notebook. In it was a list of
local farmers her father had contacted and what they had
given towards the cost of a new horse for the luckless family.
"Would they have done it today?" I was asked.

Some famous Dales farms (still intact, though no longer
self-sufficient) are reached with effort. Among them is Cosh,
standing one and a-half miles from the head of Littondale, a
tributary of the Wharfe. Mrs Brown, a former farmer's wife,
was so "starved" of gossip she would invite any ramblers in
for a cup of tea. The strangers also gave her the latest news.
Cam Houses, standing among the lean lands, was a collection
of small farms which lay in the parish of Horton-in-
Ribblesdale. Kit Calvert, of Hawes, bought a white cow at
Cam—and, when driving it away, lost it in a blizzard. Kit had
to return the following day to look for it.

To explore (with great care) one of these derelict frontier
farms is to marvel that any family could find enough space to
live between the ragged walls where now a pair of kestrels
nests in a cavity or a pair of ring-ouzels have built their nest
beside the upstairs window. An outbarn had "tying" for
perhaps a dozen cows, which spent the winter tethered by
the neck and were milked twice daily. The milk had the
cream separated from it to be converted into butter (sold at
sixpence a pound) and the "blue" milk (now an expensive
premium health food) was given to haytime workers—or to
any pigs which were being fattened.

An outbarn stood in the meadow from which came the hay
to fill its "mewstead". Muck from the wintering cattle was
heaped up and spread in the spring of the year to revitalise
the jaded land. The cattle were "let out" to a handy water
source twice a day. A Swaledale man recalls: "When I went
to school, at Muker, I followed a track through fields and
fothered (fed) the cows. Dad followed an hour or so later and
wattered 'em."

Among the variations on the theme of High Dale dereliction are the stone cabins where, in August, the grouse-shooters assembled for the mid-day break. I know a place on Giggleswick Common where the customary two rooms (one for t'gentry and one for beaters) are linked by a shelter for the horse which was used to bring up "goodies" for lunch. A round of beef for the beaters was cooked at The Traddock, Austwick. One "Glorious Twelfth", no bread was delivered. "We had beef sandwiches," said my informant. He chuckled and added: "I slapped a piece o' fat in between two bits o' lean."

The social differences are marked even after such buildings have lost their roofs. The Giggleswick Common example has grass growing in the posh-end and nettles where the beaters used to sit. Indeed, the upper dales, once so neat and tidy, now have the unkempt appearance of a depopulated landscape. The emphasis has swung from milk to beef production, from herby grasses to conifers.

A Wharfedale man, returning after being absent for many years, said: "What a ruddy scrow (mess)."

An old-style Dales chapel was box-like and unadorned,
except for the Biblical text writ large on the wall behind
a pulpit, which in size and importance was like the
bridge of a ship, the rostrum supporting a family-size
Bible. The pews were hard—harder still, after a twenty-
minute prayer or a forty-minute sermon. The hymns
were lustily sung, to the accompaniment of harmonium
or small organ.

The Old-Style Methodism

MY GRANDFATHER was a Methodist local preacher of t'owd-fashioned sort. His faith was rock-hard. He loved to smoke a pipe but one day, while walking beside the Aire, he had a feeling that God did not want him to smoke. He took the pipe from his mouth and tossed it in the river. My father was a local preacher. He once took a service at Barden, in Wharfedale. The chapel-keeper, whose living quarters were at ground-floor level, was also the society steward and organist. As she passed the pulpit on her way to the organ, she whispered: "Cut thee sermon short when tha smells t'Yorkshire pudding."

I was a Methodist local preacher for over forty years. When I showed nervousness in a Dales vestry before the service, a steward remarked: "Nay, lad—we should be freightened o' thee. Not thee of us!" I "came off the Plan", partly in sorrow at a decision by Conference that some good friends, the auxiliaries—those who served as preachers but had not qualified—should take an examination or cease to preach. At the stroke of a pen, rural Methodism lost power and appeal.

Most of the Dales auxiliaries (who hadn't cost Methodism a penny) were hill farmers, characters to a man, some from remote holdings. Their "thees" and "thou's" were derived from t'Good Book. Their extempore prayers were apt to be repetitive and, when preaching, they were just getting into their mental stride after twenty minutes. But they spoke from the heart and from rural experience.

Many good stories are told about local preachers. When the Prodigal Son returned home, having "spent up", he had been driven to feeding swine. A Nidderdale preacher said: "And soa t'lad came 'ome agean—and he was all clarted

95

up wi' pig muck." A visiting preacher, in t'owd days, was invited to a local house for a meal. A Dales farmer's son remarked: "I know what we're going to have for dinner, mister...It's jam roly-poly pudding...Me mam's only got one stocking on." This story will be understood only by the old uns.

The local preacher who, arriving at a remote chapel, found only one person was attending, said: "Let's have a few words of prayer, brother, and then we can go home." The worshipper, a retired farmer, said: "If I'd getten a cow at t'outbarn, I'd go an' fodder it." So the local preacher, retaliating in a Christianly way, made up a service with five hymns, a prayer lasting twenty-five minutes, two lessons and a sermon of forty-five minutes." Afterwards, the farmer rose stiffly to his feet and said: "If I'd getten a cow at t'outbarn—I wouldn't give it all t'hay at once!"

The old-style preachers—"Sweet Singers of Zion"—bolstered our hopes, stoked up our fears and had a no-holds-barred approach to religion which would be refreshing today when there is little faith and hardly any constraints. I still have Methodism in my madness. And I still take services now and again a little country chapels where there are no twanging guitars and action-songs.

One of them is Harrop, tucked away in a quiet part of Bowland and reached along a gated cul-de-sac. At Harrop, the congregation is composed mainly of farmfolk; the organist plays a harmonium and on cold days the steward lights a coal fire in an open grate. Afterwards, the fellowship is continued over a cup o' tea at the nearest farmhouse. At Timble, in the Washburn Valley, where I was invited to conduct a harvest festival, candles and oil lamps augmented the feeble daylight and the hymn-singing was accompanied by a lady who strummed the keys of a battery-operated Yamaha.

At Mount Zion, Tosside, a chapel of the Old Independency, which is now open for worship but four times a year, I occupied a pulpit so lofty it was like being on the bridge of a small coaster. In the centre of the chapel, a huge coke stove glowed white hot in the gloom. The bride at a wedding had walked so close to the stove that her veil was drawn to it and frizzled.

For seven years, in the 1950s, home was the village of Austwick. At the red-roofed chapel, built largely through the efforts of the Byles family, who came from Bradford, the organ was hand-pumped, with old Mr Batty as the organ-blower. His guide as to how much air remained in the bellows was a piece of lead, dangling on a string, with the words "empty" and "full" marked on the adjacent wood-work. Above the word "full" some wit had scribbled "bust".

Methodists like a good sing, especially to a familiar tune. Malcolm Skidmore, who is well-known throughout the Dales as an auctioneer, told me the story of the preacher who, hearing unfamiliar strains from the harmonium, said to the lady organist: "Can we have a more up-to-date tune?" She replied: "You can't have anything more up-to-date than this. I'm makkin' it up as I goes on." The new book *Hymns and Psalms,* a most substantial compilation, is not yet used at all the Dales chapels. The steward at Ingleton asked me about it, smiled and remarked: "They tell me it's a block-and-tackle job."

We had our moments of high emotion at Austwick when a local quarryman uttered rousing "Hallelujahs" and "Amens" if a preacher made a particularly telling point. The quarryman sometimes disagreed with what was being said, and in this case he shouted: "No, lord". I was heckled at Keasden, in the days of full chapels and attentive worshippers, when I made the mistake of telling a fanciful children's address. It did not appeal to the realistic elders, one of whom yelled: "We want none o' thee fairy tales here!" It was these same men who, if they disagreed with something a preacher had said during his sermon, afterwards discussed it with him in the vestry.

After almost two hundred years of powerful witness in the

Dales, Methodism is waning. At some chapels a lively fellowship remains. At many others, on Sunday, the footfalls of the Faithful Few rouse the echoes. Many chapels have closed. Barden chapel, where my father brought his sermon to a close when he smelt t'Yorkshire pudding, is now a craft centre.

The Barbers Who Arrived in July

LUKE CASEY, presenter of *The Dales Diary,* a popular television series, told me he was born and reared in County Mayo. Most of the Irish haytime workers who visited the Dales in summer came from that part of Ireland. They were known as the July Barbers.

Irish haytime men were numerous up to the 1914-18 war. Conditions in western Ireland were fairly good but the farms were small, families were large and a man might leave his (pregnant) wife to attend to the home acres while he—and any big sons—travelled by rail and boat to England, offering their haytime skills for a month at a fixed sum, which included food and lodging.

The July Barbers continued to arrive, though on a dwindling scale, until the mid-1950s, by which time the Dales farms were almost fully mechanised. An Aptrick (Appletreewick) farmer hired one of the last of the migrant labourers in 1957. This man, who was in his mid-fifties, had thirteen children, including nine sons of working age.

Irishmen waiting to be hired in Bentham, Skipton and Hawes were usually conspicuous but a brother-in-law of mine, who had a large farm, was somewhat upset at Skipton when a stranger, noticing a tinge of redness about his hair, approached him and said: "Is ta for hire?" Kit Calvert, of Hawes, had many tales of July Barbers. Some of the men made directly for the farms where they had previously been hired. Such a man had become "yan o' t'family." Others had to wait to be noticed. Kit said: "T'awd farmers used to waddle away wi' their walking sticks, passing some of the Irishmen and looking at 'em as though they were sheep in a pen at t'auction mart."

A farmer said to a likely lad: "Is ta hirin?" "Aye". The deal was "fixed" by a "luck penny" (usually half a crown). Prior to 1914, a month's wage was £4 or £5, though a man who had a continually dry throat might accept a pound less if there was plenty of beer. A gallon of ale was taken into the meadow whenever Irishmen were set to work.

In the early 1930s, the going rate was the equivalent of £8.50. A Dales farmer who paid a man this sum was grieved when the weather turned stormy. "I hired him for a month and we hadn't got out of t'Home Field when t'month was up. He left me standing—and took me £8.50. I didn't blame him. He was going east to help with the harvest."

An Irishman was usually regarded as one of the family, though it was not unknown for some to be accommodated in an outbuilding—in one case a glorified hen hut which the farmer's wife tried to make homely by putting up some pictures. One, an oil painting which had "come down" in the family, was hastily returned to the house when a visitor said it might be valuable. It was.

The Irish Barbers excelled as scythesmen in an age when meadow grass was felled by scythe, a typical blade—six feet long—being kept sharp by application of the strickle. This was a piece of wood, pitted with holes. Fat was rubbed on to the strickle, which was then dusted with a fine, hard sand collected from the shore of one of the upland tarns. The sand worked its way into the holes, where it was held by the fat, providing an abrasive surface. An Irishman who was "verra particular" brought his own scythe, arriving with the blade tied to the pole.

In the upper dales, the Irishmen's pride in their ability to use the scythe led to a (non-Methodist) farmer allowing men from surrounding farms to "have a go" in a meadow on a competitive basis, the chosen day being a Sunday when normal work was in abeyance. The audience consisted of local people gambling on who was the smartest worker.

When haytime was labour-intensive, good workers were at

a premium. Some Irishmen were good at loading the horse-drawn sledges being used on upland farms. Others excelled at forking hay into the barns. At a Craven farm, it was discovered that the Irish contingent included a champion whiskey-distiller. The farmer said: "Leave t'hay alone. We can manage that. Just tell me what you want for makkin' whiskey—and I'll get it." The home-made still lay among the lumber in an outbuilding till recently.

Bob o' Cam, who lived at the head of Wharfedale, employed two or three Irishmen for a hay season's work. He bought eight sixteen-gallon barrels of ale at a special low rate of "six bob a barrel". Said Bob, wonderingly: "Ale's cheaper na tea." Irish workers were prone to don too many clothes. Mary Boothman, who used to farm at Coniston Cold, told me of an Irishman who dropped dead through heatstroke. The other two Irishmen refused to do any more work; they had their own form of wake, with lots of drink.

On Saturday night, begrimed and weary Irishman went to bed, to re-emerge from lodgings next morning in his best clothes—blue suit, white shirt, smart tie, cap and brown boots—ready to walk to the nearest Catholic Church to attend Mass. Several generations of an Irish family might help with haytime on a Dales farm and became virtually members of the family.

When one man, now getting old, decided he could no longer visit the Dales in summer, the farmer dropped him a note and said he proposed to call on him in his west-Irish farm. Having only a few days to spare, the dalesman had a protracted journey—train to Stranraer, boat to Larne and the (not always punctual) Irish trains to the far west. He arrived at his old friend's farm only a few hours after his letter had been delivered and with only two hours to spend there before he had to begin the protracted return journey to the Dales.

Ten years ago, wishing to know more about County Mayo, from which most of our Dales haytime helpers came, I drove through the area, with its storm-scrubbed mountains, gleaming lakes and the island of Achill, the largest off Ireland, and now tethered to the mainland by a metal bridge. On Achill, a boatman prepared to launch his curragh, which is fashioned of light wood and tarred canvas. He seemed a typical local fisherman, with dark jacket and trousers, a well-knitted blue jumper and cap with a neb. He teased me when I mentioned about Achill's distinction as the largest island off Ireland. There was another contender for this title—England!

I had hoped for a chat about life in County Mayo, and about the summer emigration of haytime workers to the Dales, but this Mayo man—like Luke Casey, the television presenter—had spent much of his working life in northern England.

Walter Morrison's "Mountain Home"

WALTER Morrison was the fifth of seven sons of James Morrison, who amassed a fortune as a draper and on his death was a millionaire four times over. Walter, born in London on May 21, 1836, was at Eton and Balliol, undertook the Grand Tour, which he extended to take in Egypt, Syria and the United States, and (on his 21st birthday) inherited the Malham Tarn Estate from his father. His appeal to the dalesfolk rested partly on his status as a millionaire. He was also renowned as a man who made "brass"—and hung on to it! Morrison had homes in London and Devonshire but for many years he summered on the Moor, over 1,000 ft above sea level. He referred to Malham Tarn House as "my mountain home".

His return to Malhamdale was always announced by a telegraph received at Malham Post Office, whereupon the Misses Baines wended their weary, sometimes painful way, to the Tarn. It is recalled by one of the gamekeeper's daughters that the Baines sisters "had a little terrier and it seemed to enjoy the walk more than they did...It made for the Kennels and upset all our dogs...The telegram was left at our house. Grannie used to make the Misses Baines a cup of tea and she'd tell 'em: 'One of t'kids 'll tak yon telegram up to t'hall'."

Morrison could easily have afforded transport from the railway station at Bell Busk or Settle to Malham Tarn but—a fresh air fanatic since his youth—he preferred to walk and did so at a steady, mile-eating pace. Morrison, as a pedestrian, is recalled as "a big man, baldish on top, with a bushy beard" who walked with his hands behind his back and his chest sticking out. This tall, stiffly-built man with the bent head was recognisable at a range of half a mile. He tended to wear formal clothes, with a square shaped grey flat hat. He was recalled by a visitor for grouse-shooting as having "a round, jovial face with brindled whiskers." Morrison was known to call at a shop in Settle and buy a leg of mutton, which he bore triumphantly home. During his walk, on an unmetalled road which was dusty in dry weather and puddly in rain, he was indifferent to other people and "seemed to be living in a world of his own.

In subsequent walks, he was solitary but not lonely for hours, trudging through the area where the only sounds were the bleating of the horned sheep and the calls of the upland waders, including curlew and lapwing. Morrison's estate lay at the southern rim of the largest outcrop of limestone in Britain. He gloried in the cliffs, gorges and outcrops that brightened up a a landscape licked smooth by wind and rain.

Morrison was not averse to riding when the spirit moved him. He would instruct his coachman, Robert Battersby, to prepare the horse and landau and off they would go. In the early days, when Morrison was known to stay at the Tarn for Christmas, he was being taken for a horse-and-carriage ride, with Battersby and his butler, Skirrow, on the box, when they noticed an inebriated postman lying beside the road. At Morrison's insistence, the carriage was stopped. Skirrow told the vowel-slurring postman to say as little as possible or he would incriminate himself. Morrison, when told the poor man had an exacting round and was ill, promptly wrote to the General Post Office suggesting that they cut down on his duties.

His "mountain home" stood on a man-made ledge above the Tarn which had its level raised four feet when the Listers dammed it in 1791. Morrison was not averse to tinkering with the landscape, though a scheme of electrification, using water from the Tarn, was not carried out. The idea was to instal a ram to pump water to a dam on the scars, from which it would flow back into the Tarn via a turbine. Judged by modern standards, Malham Tarn House was bare and comfortless. "Walter Morrison never seemed to notice or care for comforts," wrote a neighbour, Geoffrey Dawson (who was Editor of *The Times*). "Yet, like Morrison himself, it was solid and substantial...with big rooms, big windows and a big outlook." When the House was damaged by fire in 1873, Morrison soon had the place restored. Being Morrison, that work "was carried on with alacrity".

Morrison rejoiced in the freshness of the "mountain" air. As a young man with consumption, he had been sent by the doctors to Pau, "a very malarious district under the Pyrenees." He insisted on going up to the snow line, despite the doctor's comment that if he did, he would be dead in forty-eight hours. Not only did Morrison remain alive he "discovered that fresh pure air is good for consumption before any doctor found it out." Later in life, when ill, he told a friend: "I do not take medicine." He considered using the "ozone" treatment for wounds, which would lead to the discarding of bandages.

William Skirrow, the butler, presided over the house in Cromwell Road, London, and travelled to Malham Tarn House when required. Mrs Skirrow, housekeeper, was the former Martha Duxbury, of Settle. Her brother had a confectionery business in Cheapside. Martha was so house-proud that her staff said that spring-cleaning was almost a daily occurrence. Miss Lodge, housekeeper, washed and polished the pieces of coal (Derby Brights) before they were placed in the scuttle for Mr Morrison's drawing room. Alfred Ward (gamekeeper) became engaged to Ellen Earnshaw (cook) and then told Walter Morrison he would have to leave for a job with a better cottage than he had. Morrison's prompt reaction was to provide a splendid house called Sandhills.

Morrison's mountain estate bustled under the agent, John Whittingale Winskill, who achieved a great deal with virtually no back-up in the shape of an assistant or clerk; who was a dapper-dresser and always touched (pleased) when his worth was acknowledged. Winskill's range of interests extended from tree planting to establishing a trout hatchery for the replenishment of the fish stock in the Tarn. The front lawn of the House was mown by a machine drawn by a pony called Happy Jack. Small leather shoes were placed over the iron shoes so they would not mark the lawn.

In later years, the corpulent Morrison had difficulty in clambering into the standard horse-drawn vehicles and so he was taken for a ride on the Estate by Robert Battersby using a small, four-wheeled carriage which one of the Ward lads called a "chariot". Drawn by a single horse, it enabled the great man to tour without having the reek of a car's exhaust in his nostrils. Morrison denounced motor cars as nothing but "toys of the idle rich". The time came when even he became mechanised. His first outright purchase (as opposed to having a car on hire) was a Fiat, which he acquired from Billy Slinger, a mechanical genius and eccentric.

I was told by Fred Ellis, a local garage proprietor, that Walter didn't intend to drive the car himself, so he sent Battersby, his coachman, then aged 75, to Billy for driving lessons. Billy soon lost his patience, and if Battersby was not driving well he would rebuke him by kicking his foot off the clutch." After two or three circuits of the town, the old man was judged proficient at driving a car. He who had arrived in Settle by horse and carriage now returned at the wheel of a Fiat. It is said that when he arrived almost at the place where the horses turned to go into the yard, he shouted: "Whooa, lass! Whooa!" The car did not stop—it travelled straight ahead, crashing into a gatepost and smashing one of the lamps.

In 1921, after years of much public service and private philanthropy, and after a spell of indifferent health, Morrison died at a house in Sidmouth he had bought the previous year. He was buried in the yard at Kirkby Malham Church, a few miles from his "mountain home". His workmen had already collected a large flat stone from Penyghent. It was now inscribed by Jim Hodkin, the estate mason. His oaken coffin was plain and unpolished, with heavy brass fittings. It was lowered into a plain earth grave.

A newspaper correspondent wrote: "The day was bleak and dour, as though Nature herself joined in the expressions of sympathy for the death of one who loved her second to none."

The field barn held perhaps a dozen overwintering cows and the hay to sustain them. Invariably built on a bank, the barns allowed easy forking of hay into storage at one end and easy forking of the cow's dung through a forking hole at the other end. The dung was spread on the meadows to ensure another good crop of hay. Many field barns, having become redundant, have been stripped of their valuable slates to be incorporated in modern buildings.

The Little Dalehead Barns

HUNDREDS of small, stone-and-slate barns give dignity and much interest to an upper Dales landscape which has for centuries been devoted to the rearing of stock. Nowhere are the barns seen in greater number and diversity than in upper Swaledale, where fifty or sixty might be counted in a stretch two miles long.

No two barns appear to be exactly alike. There is an underlying plan, but the quality of the workmanship varies. Some have great character and others have the design spoilt by an additional shippon, with (now rusting) corrugated roof. Yet more are basic, consisting of just the barn, a mewstead, a baulks and a shippon for six over-wintering stirks. One barn was built on a sloping rock shelf and storage space was limited.

The masonry on some barns was mortared and others were built dry. Further down the dale were field barns incorporating much dressed stone and with ornamental cornices protruding like wings. A barn built of rubble could not be recycled, as when the material was used for walling.

The first barns were simple, modest in size, with high gables to support beams and thatch. Such a barn survived until recent times at Hurst, above Swaledale. Barns with crucks had thatched roofs which were so steep that when the thatch (of ling stalks) was to be replaced, this was done with corrugated iron. Ordinary slates would not "stick". A useful guide to the age of a later barn is the woodwork. If the beams have been chopped or split, they are of early date. Beams which have been neatly sawn usually date from the nineteenth century. They must be strong because many a barn was roofed with slates up to an inch and a-half thick.

The best of the Craven barns are noted for their handsome porches—big enough for a cart laden with hay to be left under cover overnight to "save" the hay from an unexpected downpour. A good porch also provided shelter for stock if the weather was inclement. The meaner structures of the upper dale might also have the stub of a porch. Pat Evoy thinks that in some cases this was to protect (from the weather) the large doors of the barn. They had to be bought in and would be very expensive, especially if made of oak. A door which originally was of pegged oak had parts of it renewed in softwood to avoid the expense of replacement.

With every little barn distinctive (while conforming to a basic design), the minor features are of special interest. In a wall of the porch there might be a recess—a storage space where even a three-legged stool might be kept. The building was more precisely known as coo's (cowhouse). The milk was transported to the farmhouse by back-can, which held about six gallons. When milking, it was customary to have the pail in the left hand and stool in the right hand or the cow would be fretful enough to kick out. That was the way it had always been done! If two cows were standing side by side— which they did, each tethered to a boskin-stick and with a stick between them to prevent them from turning round— you had to squeeze between 'em.

A barn is gloomy, mysterious, the beams draped with cobwebs. A barn owl perched on a beam looks down at you before flying out through a forking hole. A big barn has a threshing floor between the double-doors and a single door on the facing wall. The through draught which occurred on a breezy day with both doors open meant that conditions were ideal for threshing. A wooden flail was brought down on the grain, which lay on an expanse of wood. The chaff blew away.

It's a long time since grain was produced on an updale farm. The field barn was a self-contained wintering unit for a few young cattle. The larger barn held proportionately more stock. The size of the mewstead (where the hay was stored) indicated how many cattle were usually kept here. On the other side of the threshing-floor was the shippon, covered over by wood known as baulks, forming a loft where the greenest of the hay was kept. Between mewstead and shippon, in the better-class barns, was a space known as a "foddergang" in which the farmer could operate comfortably while feeding the cattle.

Otherwise, the farmer had to cut himself a "gang" with his hay-knife—a job guaranteed to keep him warm on frosty days. One barn which was "all baulks" needed a special routine. The first task when the cows were being wintered was to cut the hay to a trapdoor, through which the "desses" of hay were dropped to an area handy to the shippon. In parts of North Ribblesdale and adjacent areas, barns were provided with flagged floors, the flags being of the Horton variety, quarried at Helwith Bridge.

Over-wintering cattle were in the "liggin" from November till May, lying down, two by two, in a space known as a boose. The main divisions were known as boskins. Each cow was held by a special band or tie, extending from its neck to a round iron and swivel-hank which ran up and down a "boskin stake". Urine and dung went into a channel which could be easily kept clean.

The cattle were let out periodically to drink at a trough or spring. Sometimes the stock had to go a considerable distance to drink or, as in one case, a journey of a few hundred yards which involved negotiating steep ground to reach the beck. A Swaledale farmer recalled that in his schooldays he walked from Angram to Muker via the field barns, feeding hay to the cows. His father followed-on, letting the stock out to water. Arthur Young, visiting Swaledale in the latter part of the eighteenth century, noted that in winter the cows were fed on hay alone, "of which they eat one and a-half acre per head."

The little dalehead field barns were an integral part of a

111

fellside culture evolved by a hard-working, self-reliant, thrifty people. A barn stood in a field which (this being the Dales) was invariably sloping. On the upperside of the building was the "mew". Hay might be forked through a hole using a fork with a shaft of moderate length and with a minimum of effort. In winter, the hay could be moved downwards to the shippon where the cattle stood and, also "downbank", was the muck-hole, leading directly to the middenstead outside; this was cleared every fortnight or so in dry weather to get rid of it and also to revive the jaded meadows.

The muck was put out in heaps—meticulously placed heaps, resembling "an army on parade"—and subsequently "scaled" with a fork when a convenient time arrived. So a field barn might, theoretically, be worked by one man, one horse and a variety of sleds or carts.

The farmer wanted a supply of hay as fodder, bracken and sieves (rushes) as bedding. In "chancy" weather, he had sometimes to take his hay on the green side. Then the danger was of excess sweating, leading to spontaneous combustion and—fire. So the "mew" was invariably built up during haytime with a sweat-pole up the middle. Pat McEvoy recalls when a bag was used, being raised according to the height of the mew until there was a sweat-hole "to let the steam out". When green hay had dried a bit, it was white over with mould, but though the top of the hay would be a bit rotten, underneath it was "rather like silage, which is 'pickled grass' as opposed to hay, or 'dry grass'. This fodder was rich and brown, resembling tobacco. The cows loved it."

The dry-cows and stirks at the little barns lived on virtually nothing but hay; the milk cows would get a little provender as well. The quality of the hay varied a good deal, which was why the hay was cut down into desses, to mix up the poor hay on top where it had sweated or in the bottom, where it was damp from the ground. In between the quality was mixed—some good, some from "rakings", which was always poor quality stuff. Pat found that the quality of hay governed the amount of milk given by dairy cows much more than the quality of provender which was given.

Barns were unofficial dormitories for tramps, some of whom, having received food and drink from the Dales families, went off to an isolated barn to sleep. One tramp ran the risk of decapitation from a hay-spade being used by a farmer who had no idea the man was in the building. He stopped work when he saw an arm being frantically waved as the tramp awoke.

The barn was home to a stray cat. Hedgehogs found them ideal places in which to hibernate. Pat Evoy remembers handling his hay with care and, in some cases, re-housing hedgehogs so they would survive the winter.

Scattered about the Dales, up to an elevation of 1,650 ft., with one at the top of Apedale, another by t'Buttertubs Pass and several between West Stonesdale and Tan Hill, are the 1960s successors of the lile stone barns. Railway wagons, of the covered variety, with sliding doors, and now minus their wheels, were purchased for £25 each and set down on the open landscape as durable storage places for hay and provender.

Meanwhile, where dairy farming still exists, the cows work on the feed-when-you're-hungry system, housed in an open shed, with an adjacent silage heap the cattle will champ their way through during the winter.

It's less cosy, and infinitely less romantic, than the field barns.

Autumn Into Winter

A COMMON WREN

In the west and north of Yorkshire are the dalesfolk, who wring their hard living from the Pennines with its bleak soil and grim weather.

...In the autumn sunshine, the play of light on the low hills and the chasing cloud shadows over the high fell-tops give a wonderful sense of spaciousness.

Harry J Scott (1965).

Visitor: "Does it always rain?"
Dales farmer: "Sometimes it snaws."

Evenings with Barn Owls

YOU WILL have heard the story of the dalesman and a friend from the city who were walking at the "edge of dark" when a weird sound was heard. The city man queried which creature had made such a blood-curdling sound. The dalesman said it was an owl. "I know that," was the reply, "but what was 'owling?" If any bird sound is calculated to send six-inch shivers down the spine of a stranger, it is that of the barn owl—an owl which flies through the half-light like a big white moth.

I spent many an evening watching barn owls before the lusty growth of one of our brave new conifer forests could clag the landscape with an impenetrable mass of trees and deprive the good earth of light. Such forestland is seen in Widdale, near Hawes, and in a great arc around the northern side of Penyghent. In the forest I visited (with permission, of course) several owl pairs were nesting in old farmsteads and barns which stood incongruously with a stubble of young sitka spruce around them. The birds I watched were in a small barn right at the edge of the forest. The adult birds divided their food-hunting time between the dark alleys between the trees and rough pastureland visited by scarcely any creature but sheep and nesting birds.

The forest was benevolent to owls. It rustled with short-tailed field voles whose runs, canopied by the ungrazed grass, were to be found everywhere. The voles left piles of bright green droppings as a minute offering to the fertility of the ground. I used a hide of wood and hessian which could be approached, latterly on all-fours, through an area of well-grown trees. It was a matter of personal pride to enter the hide and settle down for a vigil without hearing the pathetic

115

alarm squeal of an adult bird. In the early evening, stimulated into activity by the hunger cries of the young, the adults put in an appearance. I expected to see the cock bird first; it perched on a window ledge, shuffling its feathers while it blinked the last of the sleep mist from its lustrous eyes.

There were evenings of brilliant sunlight and evenings when the rain fell as though from a celestial hosepipe. Hours later, when the summer sun re-appeared, the forest steamed. I settled in the hide with binoculars, coffee in a flask and midge cream in a handy dispenser. On the warm, still evenings, the midges danced in the air like wreaths of brown smoke. And if I were to kill a midge, a hundred of its friends turned up for the funeral. The hunger-cries of the owlets formed a light, rhythmic "snoring" which seemed to be synchronised to the slow beating of my heart. When little was happening, I fought hard to stay awake! I stared at the barn through a hole cut in the hessian. By moving on my wooden seat (an old beer crate) I could scan an area of rushy ground near the barn and also, by turning my head, the nearest forest "ride".

The light snoring of the owlets continued. I tried to shake off the desire to slumber by watching a kestrel as it hovered over the dark green pyramids of spruce. Ten minutes later, the snoring from the barn became irregular and then it stopped. The vacuum in bird interest was filled by a chevron of oystercatchers high overhead and by the beginning of what would be a considerable movement of gulls to a roost on water just over the hill. The last of the sunlight edged the gulls' white feathers with a rosy hue. At 7.35 the owlets were snoring again. The sound was quelled by a tattoo of raindrops as a cloud tinted battleship-grey cruised overhead, with a westerly wind providing the motive power. The owlets renewed their calling and the hint was taken by the cock bird.

When my eyes were prickling with the fatigue of staring at the ledge of a "forking hole", the nearest opening to the owl nest, the bird was suddenly there—an apparition in white, its wings buff and mottled with grey, staring at the forest with eyes like black grapes set in a heart-shaped facial disc, above the hooked beak which marked out the bird as a predator. This bird was darker than many barn owls I had seen. Its feathers looked ragged after weeks of attending to the young. Because its long, slender neck was swaddled in soft feathers, it was not easy to see where the head ended and the body began until it looked around. The head revolved as though on castors. The eyes of a barn owl are fixed in their sockets. Because of their large size, they provide good binocular vision for the rapid descent on to prey, but make it necessary for the neck to be turned if the owl is to look around.

When the cock owl had flown off, beating along the ride in a silent flight which gave its hearing a chance to function without undue distraction, I pondered on the unseen family, which would be of disproportionate sizes. The hen bird began incubation when the first egg was laid; more eggs appeared at two-day intervals and so there was a gap of over a week between the oldest and the youngest. The youngster which appeared to view had gone through two moults in the nest and was now in adult plumage.

The cock bird returned, flying across the glade with shallow wingbeats, clutching at a vole with talons that can instantly crush life from small bodies. On this occasion, the luckless vole was still squeakingly alive. The bird alight on the ledge; transferred the vole neatly from claws to beak and then flew inwards and upwards, its arrival indicated by the increased volume and pitch of the snoring of the remaining young birds at their nesting site above the cracked ceiling. I had forgotten about the hen bird until she appeared at the ledge and joined in the search for food. A shuttle service with food continued for the next hour or so. The hunger of the owlets was appeased, though in between times they continued the weird snoring.

The feeding of the young invariably began in daylight.

There was presuamably another feeding time during the night or about dawn. In bad weather, when the air was misty and trees dripped water on to an already soaked vegetation, I did not see the owls, which seemed reticent to plunge into the mini-jungle of grasses and thus draggle their plumage. On the last day of my vigil, as summer died, an orange-red sun was setting in the light grey of mist which its heat had coaxed from a wet countryside. The air was equatorially humid. A young owl showed itself on the window ledge at 8.47. Others appeared. They almost savaged the returning adults.

I will long remember the first flighting of the young owls because two of them left the barn and alighted on my hide. I was sitting with my head within a foot of where their talons had pierced the hessian. As I left for home, along a forest road, the beams of my car's headlamps revealed a barn owl hunting low. Many a barn owl has perished through colliding with high-speed traffic on motorways.

Owls no longer nest in the old barn at the edge of the forest. The building was demolished. The forest is now so tall and dense I would find difficulty in moving through it without having the clothes ripped off my back. Nesting sites for barn owls have declined and so has the owl population: by seventy per cent in the past sixty years. The last bird I saw had hungered to death in a severe winter and its emaciated body was picked up in a Dales garden.

Purple-Headed Moorland

A CALLUNA moor, with its low horizons, its peat, ling, sphagnum bog and mist, is not everyone's favourite landscape. To dalesmen like Thomas Joy of Grassington and Bill Alderson of Swaledale—Big Bill to his friends—the local moor was almost as familiar as the home parlour. Such men have talked to me incessantly about t'moor, its life and traditions.

Thomas told me that Grassington Moor has "nine hundred acres of heather and t'same again of mosscrop", which is a sedge known as "cotton grass". It whitens the upland plateaux as though with summer snow. Early in the year, sheep "push their noses between the bent-grass, seeking the emergent mosscrop, which is white, tender and sweet." What they don't eat develops into what Thomas called a "fuzzy yellow top" and, in due course, into the familiar blob of "cotton".

Heather grows best on the dry ridges, giving the late summer spectacle of purple-headed moorland as the ling comes into bloom. The diminutive purple flower is bell-shaped, one of a cluster hanging in loose spikes. Collectively, the flowering ling is tonally strong enough to stain the under-bellies of the clouds. Swaledale has some of the finest moors in Britain—acid moors, strong in tone, with low horizons but majestic in their extent. When they are empurpled, a walker across a succession of ridges might—in a particularly dry time—kick up white clouds of heather pollen, fine as dust, at every footfall.

Most of the windows of Bill's farmhouse at Angram framed views of the moors, which could be broody for months on end, only to crackle into life with the beginning of grouse-shooting in August. Bill's family ran sheep on the moors and took peat off them to keep the home fires burning. There was so much dust from peat that a Swaledale farmer, when cleaning out the ass-'oil (ash-hole) under the fire used to back a horse and cart up to the kitchen door and use a big shovel. The subsequent heap attracted hens in the mood for a dust-bath.

Bill had sometimes been lost, as when mist came down unexpectedly, "but I've allus fun (found) missen. I've kept going till I fun somewhere I knew. At times, I've bin a bit surprised at where I came out..." When the Glorious Twelfth of August arrived, and the "nobs" turned up for the opening of the grouse-shooting season, the Aldersons and other updale families provided a back-up—labour needed as beaters, plus a Dales pony to "move stuff to t'moor" and convey the slain birds from it.

Bill was familiar with two sooarts o' grouse. There is the red grouse, which everyone knows, if only from pictures in books or corpses at the poulterer's shop. The red grouse is found on black (peaty) ground. Its cousin, the black grouse, which was described to me as "big as a littleish turkey", occurs mainly on t'white grund, which is the marginal ground where grasses like *Nardus stricta* predominate.

Bill "wasn't struck" on the taste of red grouse. A relative of his wife who cooked at the big house when the lord of the manor was in residence used to relate: "They hanged yon grouse till they dropped off bi t'heeads. They were bad—but some folk still ate 'em." Black grouse make good eating and, according to Bill, have three different colours o' meat—"pink and white and then rather dark. They're solid birds." I asked him how they were cooked. "Difference o' ways—same as owt else," he replied.

By the time the red grouse had been stirred up a few times by poachers, including men working with nets (a silent way of catching birds at night), the birds were nervous and wary of being driven to the guns. "You couldn't get near 'em.

They'd get up hundreds of yards away. Or as soon as they saw you. At back-end, they formed packs till there seemed to be thousands. I've seen t'sky black wi' 'em as they went over t'butts." The population throve and flagged in cycles of five years or so.

Bill's special stamping grounds in August were moors belonging to the Keld estate where, in his early days, the lessee for three years was Major Hubert Martineau. (The shooting lodge is now Keld youth hostel. Before it was built, shooters were accommodated at Kirkby Stephen and transported to the moors by wagonette). The Major and his friends shot till the barrels of the guns were red hot, bagging up to 500 brace a day. "In those days there was some stir about Keld."

Local men fell out with each in the scramble to be taken on as beaters. The going rate was six shillings a day, with a further six shillings for anyone who arrived with a Dales pony. The pony attendant must not be scruffy. "He had to dress reight and put on a collar and tie. Gentry didn't want him dressed onnyroad..."

Big Bill was wrily amused by the manner and antics of the visitors to the Moors. "I used to carry (guns) for an American woman till I got fed up. She was bad to deal wi'. I used to have a job to git her on to t'hoss. Skirts were ower-tight at t'start. She couldn't git on. Then she was loaded up wi' guns and cameras and bags and cigarettes. They were them sweet 'uns. She filled a bag wi' cigarettes every day. She did give a lot out to lads."

Bill usually had a job transporting grouse to the bird-house. "They used to kill four thousand to five thousand brace in a season, just on those Keld moors. I had a horse with panniers on its back. Grouse were packed in tight—each bird with its head under a wing—to make 'em compact. There was space in t'panniers for about fifty brace...At the bird house they were laid with their heads over t'sides of shelves."

Next morning, a carrier came for them in good time; "he

121

was coming up the dale before five o' clock, being in a hurry to get 'em off to London. Aye—he took 'em to Richmond and put 'em on an early train.''

Major J E E Yorke, while staying with his grandfather—t'Owd Squire—at Bewerley Hall in Nidderdale, acquired sharp memories of grouse-shooting in the days before new moorland tracks and Land Rovers speeded the shooters to the butts. There was a vehicle—''a huge wagonette, drawn by two horses.'' Being very young at the time, he was allowed to sit on the box, ''but I was belted to the rail in case I fell.'' The loaders travelled in another wagonette but had to walk for a good deal of the way.

The moors were well managed. Burning ensured there was always fresh young growth, food for the grouse and the sheep, but old heather was left here and there against the time the moor was overblown with snow. ''The sheep, moving in this long heather, left paths that the grouse might follow.'' Tom Simpson, the head keeper, had such an amazingly sharp eye for grouse on the wing he would arrange for his under-keepers to drive grouse along flight lines and would cull the old birds, identifiable by little more than the bold red wattles and the darkness of the plumage, in October.

Some estate workers lived in remote places. Major Yorke chatted with a man who had a large family. His neighbour had also produced many children. ''Aye,'' said the first man, ''we haddent so much to do up here of a winter's neet. It's different nah—they've got telly.'' A gamekeeper did not receive much money as such but was usually content to have a secure job with house, rent, rates, perhaps a pig and certainly a garden.

Many Dales moors were wrecked by overstocking with sheep during the 1939-45 war. Modern moors are beset by tick, heather beetle and the insidious spread of bracken.

Pioneers of Re-cycling

HARDLY anything is "chucked away" on a Dales farm. "It'll come in," says the farmer. His wife reminds him he has still to find a use for the twelve toilet seats he bought at a sale. Old iron bedheads spanned gaps in a lazy farmer's walls—until someone told the owners that such items, with their superb brass top-pieces, were "collector's pieces" and valuable.

A Dales auctioneer finds a customer for virtually everything—except a second-hand wardrobe, relatively new and therefore of no value for its wood content. There might be half a dozen wardrobes available at give-away prices. At one sale, a man bought every wardrobe in sight. The auctioneer beamed. He would not have to arrange for their disposal. The purchaser said: "Thou can tak that smile off thee face. I'se nobbut having t'best 'un and I'm leaving t'rest."

The first tractors to reach the upper dales were Fordsons, which during the war turned many an old meadow "brown side up" as part of the compulsory ploughing programme. From 1946, the little grey Ferguson was the "workhorse" on the Dales farms. Yet in the 1920s and 1930s, long before a pure-bred tractor appeared, there were Land Cars—motorised mowers, made from re-cycled cars, stripped down, with a mowing machine—a quite ordinary machine, of the sort drawn by horses but minus the shaft—chain-driven from the back axle. An old farmer told Rufus Carr, who made many a Land Car from Austin 12 cars he stripped down, "Eh—it'll never mow like a couple o' horses." But it did—as the farmer and a friend saw when, esconsed behind a hedge, they watched Rufus testing it.

The Austin 12 was a favourite because of its weight and four cylinder petrol engine. Rufus bought a car at a scrapyard for as little as 17s.6d and the mowing-machine, complete, was sold for £17. The purchaser was given a five-gallon drum of oil as a bonus. Some mowers lasted for ten years and more. He bought over 50 old Austins at one scrapyard in a year and with the help of a lad did the work of modification; his brother's wife tested out a mower before it was delivered. (A do-it-yourself conversion job at Clapham worked but no allowance had been made for the comfort of the driver, who sat bolt upright against a block of wood and had to be virtually prised out of the seat when the working day was over).

Rufus also put two gear boxes in an old Austin 12 motor and used it as a small-farm tractor. Farmers used it for all sorts of jobs, including muck-leading. He put a plough on the back of one of them as a special order. The efficiency was increased when each back wheel was provided with two tyres—the normal tyre and another which fitted over it. The wire rim of this additional tyre was cut off, and slots were made for extra gripping.

Never throw away a piece of binder-twine. That will certainly "come in". I've seen twine holding up a farmer's breeches. It is widely used for fettling-up (repairing) gates and, in the case of a farmer with a broken ankle who was told not to get the plaster wet, twine was wrapped several times round the plastic bag he slipped over the injured limb.

A triumph of re-cycling is the Welly Gate. The first I saw was near Austwick, twenty years ago. One or two good examples are to be seen in Dentdale. And there's one—perhaps even two or three—at the field divisions where the Pennine Way heads through Gayle towards Hawes, in Wensleydale.

You may have seen a Welly Gate attached to an old-fashioned stile in a wall. It's a small gate, designed not so much to restrict walkers as to deter footloose sheep, which otherwise would squeeze through the gap from one field to another. It depends for its effectiveness on the soles of redundant wellies—soles which are cut away and used on the gate as hinges. You apply pressure to the gate to open it. The gate closes behind you with a decisive clunk. There is no awkward fastener—such as a chain with a hook on it or one of those two-piece connections which, if not working smoothly, remove a couple of inches of skin from a finger.

A variation on the theme is what I call the Dunlop Gate. Instead of using welly soles, the farmer has cut bits from an old motor tyre as hinges for the gate. It also has the strength and elasticity to keep a stile gate tightly shut. A length taken from a huge, circular tractor tyre may be used as feeding trough.

Now we are in the age of Big Bag Silage, there's less binder-twine to account for. The grass is taken green, baled and slipped into a large plastic bag to exclude the air. In a wet summer, each bag may also hold a gallon or two of water. The silage looks repulsive, but the cattle enjoy it. And that, as they say, is the object of the game.

Once the high ground held rainwater like a giant sponge, releasing it gradually. The peat was juicy, the sphagnum mosses extensive. When a "freshet" occurred, there would be high water for days on end. Drainage of various kinds—not least the "gripping" of the moors to lower the water table—now means there is a rapid run-off and an equally rapid fall in the level of a river. In times of drought, the headwaters tend to dry out until there is just a lifeless expanse of bleached stones.

A Welcome for the Salmon

THE SALMON are running. A thirteen and a-half pounder has been lifted from Long Preston Deeps. Fish have used the salmon-ladders, two series of man-made pools beside the weirs at Settle and Langcliffe. An ingenious counting device records their passage. At Stainforth Foss, my favourite vantage point, a gleam of silver is seen where a salmon has accepted the challenge of a limestone cill, a hindrance on its journey to the spawning grounds in the ocean depths off Greenland and the Faroes to the gravel beds of the Ribble where eggs will be laid and fertilised.

Stainforth Foss (the latter a Norse word for waterfall) has run milk-white after heavy rain. Salmon rest up in the pools. They need a depth of water to enable them to leap an obstruction. A fish drives itself with powerful tail movements and hurls itself clear of the water, arching its back, scuttering over wet rocks and, quite often, being washed back into the pool. The salmon will try again.

The average weight of a Ribble salmon is from seven to ten pounds, though a few years ago I tasted a steak cut from a fifteen-pounder landed, after a struggle, by a man who simultaneously pulled a leg muscle and was limping for the best part of a week. He considered the suffering worth the effort of capturing such a lordly fish. At Stainforth, where a seventeenth century, single-arch bridge looks like a rainbow set in stone, the salmonid benefit from an inconspicuous sculpting by the River Authority of an exposed bed of limestone. They did the work after much wrangling with the National Park planners.

Edward Elgar, the composer, as a young man, was fond of

127

visiting Stainforth during brief holidays from Worcester. His Dales friends provided him with a framed photograph of the bridge. He is unlikely to have seen a salmon so high up the river. Elgar was partial to "potted Ribble trout". The western rivers, including Ribble and Lune, are well patronised by salmon. (Sea trout are most often seen on tributaries such as the Hodder and the Wenning). The Yorkshire rivers with polluted lower reaches will need a little more time to become a haven for The Leaper, as its Latin name implies.

Salmon run the gauntlet of fishermen and also face many natural hazards. It is, for most of them, a journey of a lifetime; they will not live to return another year. Young salmon which left the Ribble for the ocean feeding-grounds make for the areas where upwelling water brings nutrients to the surface and, in summer, the sea blooms, sustaining a rich and diverse food chain. A homecoming salmon is thought to recognise the river where it was born by the distinctive smell.

A hen salmon, reaching the natal gravel bed in the company of a cock fish, parts with a cascade of pink eggs—some nine hundred eggs for every pound of the salmon's weight—many of which settle in the red (a shallow depression) and are covered by the male, which releases the fertilising milt over them. Some hanky-panky has been noted, with a hen fish laying eggs in more than one red. In some cases, she has been in the company of another cock salmon.

Through the winter and into spring, the gravel permits a flow of clean water to reach the eggs. But maybe less than five per cent will hatch out. Winter storms wash out the redds or cover them with silt, suffocating the eggs. The enemies of salmon eggs include heron, dipper and kingfisher. Some are taken by large trout.

Jack Charlton, taking a rest from world-class football, has been delighting anglers with a television series recording his adventures with salmon. One film, shot by the Tweed, showed fish being smoked, using oak (as they do with herring at Whitby when kippering). This sequence reminded me of a visit to a remote farm in the north of Iceland where fresh-run salmon hauled out of the river a few hundred yards away, had been sliced, revealing the rich pink of the flesh, and were about to be smoked using—dried sheep dung! Blocks of compressed dung, waiting to be used, formed a heap outside the building.

Another television film in the Charlton series showed the process of stripping eggs from a ripe female, in this case not into a redd in the gravel but into a plastic bucket. They were intended for a hatchery. A River Authority workman added a few dashes of milt from a male salmon, and stirred it all up, to ensure the eggs were evenly fertilised.

In 1861, when the stock of salmon in the Ribble was affected by pollution and fishermen's greed, Charles Dickens wrote in his magazine *All the Year Round* of young fish being caught by the thousand on their way to the sea. "Shackle nets" were in use; the fish were sold to be eaten at eightpence a pound. Dickens, who had the conservationist's outlook, added: "Ye foolish fishers; ye are eating banknotes at eightpence a pound."

Salmon in the river do not feed. They occasionally take the angler's lure. Perhaps the be-feathered hook irritates them or it is instinctive to snap at what appears to be a morsel. In the old days, poachers plied their nocturnal trade with gaff and leister (a three-pronged device on a pole). When this cruel instrument was driven into the fish, the headpiece came away and, being fitted with twine, the fish could be hauled in.

To some Dales anglers, salmon are unwelcome. A retired seadog, Vice Admiral J K im Thirn, who had fishing rights at Stainforth, where now the salmon leap from a sixteen feet pool and swim grandly by, is recalled partly for his campaign, when a salmon ladder was proposed, to keep the upper reaches clear of salmon. He preferred to have a trout preserve.

Old Dalesmen Never Die

A VETERAN FARMER, of Wharfe, near Austwick, typified for many of us the indomitable Dalesman, being one of the old-fashioned, hard-working sort. He was born on a farm tucked under Moughton Hill. He lived all his life there and recalled that when he was a boy there was bracken in every field except one. He used to scramble about at the side of the gills, pulling bracken out with his hands and clearing every field except one.

Such a man—and there were hundreds of such small, wiry farmers throughout the Dales—were self-contained, devoted to their land and stock. Under them, the Dales were farmed in a time-honoured way which never took more from the land than it had received.

Dales farmers never die—they're "takken", "pass over" or, if they were Methodist bred and born, they "go to their reward." You do not hear so much about the Pearly Gates these days, though one crusty old Yorkshire farmer who passed through them was told by St Peter: "You can come in; but we're not making Yorkshire pudding for one."

In t'owd days, there was often a rapid transition between life and death. A farmer who was near death was pestered by friends. They asked to be remembered to John, Harry and Helen, who'd already "passed over". He croaked: "When I git through Heaven's gates, does ta think I'll have nowt better to do than ask for thy John, Harry and Helen?"

When it was customary for the dead person in his coffin to be viewed by friends and neighbours, a visitor attempted to cheer up the widow by saying: "He's got a smile on his face." She replied: "He doesn't knaw he's deeard yet." At a funeral service, the 23rd Psalm was being recited, with its mention of "green pastures", when an ever-realistic farmer whispered to his neighbour: "If they're owt like Ted's pastures, they could bide a bit o' good muck."

I'm getting ahead of myself with mention of a funeral. Doctors have done their best to keep people in the land of the living. They used to be thin on the ground in the upper dales, where "we dee naturally." Doctors used to cost money, though sometimes a doctor might have his visit and medication written off by being included in the tax returns under "three loads o' muck".

The doctor was "a good hand at charging", though to be fair he had to maintain a horse, trap and coachman in case he was summoned to a remote farm. Eventually, he received a "gate allowance"—something extra to compensate for the effort of opening and closing gates on the upland roads.

Dentistry was in its infancy. Do-it-yourself dentistry was practised by Old Mr Booth, of Austwick. He winced while milking a cow, went into the house, got some pliars and removed a tooth. He returned to the milking, with blood coursing from his mouth, and winced again. "Nay, I've gitten t'wrang tooth," said he, and he promptly returned to the house to attend to it. In the Clapham district, no child complained of toothache because the tooth-extraction was performed heartlessly and in unsterile conditions by the local blacksmith, who had some pincers and a horse-hair sofa. "You lay on t'sofa and there was no escape when he'd getten his knee in t'middle of thee chest."

The best of doctors performed minor operations. "Our doctor were a clever chap. He sat me at t'edge of t'kitchen table and took my tonsils out. Ay—I can still hear 'em squeak as he cut through 'em." Normally, the patient expected "summat in a bottle". There was a bottle for making him/her sweat, another for breaking up phlegm and yet another which was neutral—a solution whose chief merit was in stopping people from worrying and giving them something to talk about.

If possible, the dalesfolk were their own doctors. A well-thumbed book on human afflictions, and what to do about them, stood on the same shelf as *Sheep in Health and Disease,* or some such tome. It was not unknown for a fretful old farmer to take a swig from a bottle of sheep medicine. Dalesfolk "put up" with complaints like t'rheumatics (a term which also covered arthritis and various other pains). A farmer, like one of his fell-going sheep, was not ill for long. He either got back on his feet quickly—or he died without much fuss. This was a blessing at a busy time of the year—lambing or haymaking. I thought one bedfast farmer had a chance of rallying until his wife said: "He's lost interest in his sheep." The end was nigh.

A Dales farmer who always put his sheep first—"they depend on me; t'missus could cope on her own"—lost his wife and ended up running the house and farm by himself. He continued to raise prize-winning tups and left instructions about three fleeces, clipped from his favourite tups, which he kept in a neat bundle in the farm kitchen. "When I die," he told his solicitor, "I want yon fleeces to go into t'coffin wi' me to keep me warm."

I sat by the "bed of sickness" occupied by a farmer who had been big, strong and hot-headed in his young days and I marvelled at his decline into a little bent old man. A friend and I laughed, not at his plight, but at some of his antics when lish (alert). He'd chucked a tax inspector into t'muck midden. When a farm man was leaning on a tractor instead of working, the farmer fired a shotgun towards him and the pellets formed a pretty pattern on the upjutting exhaust pipe.

"He had a reight paddy (temper)," I was told. "One day, I was sitting in t'kitchen with him when there was a bad weather forecast on t'wireless. He picked yon wireless up and chucked it out of t'window...Electricity men who had to cut him off—he was always a bad payer—turned up after dark, did their work and scuttered off before he heard 'em."

This farmer, like many another, over-did himself. "He

didn't knaw when to stop. If he'd nowt else to do, he take a few sheep for a ride in his owd grey van." To anyone who asked about his health, he'd say: "I'se terrible mashed." His last words on this earth were: "There's nowt funny about gitting old."

A dalesman doesn't die; he simply fades away. One of the hoary tales relates to the thrifty farming couple who "lived off next to nowt." The man became ill. He asked for a candle to brighten his last hours. His wife reminded him of the price of candles. He pleaded with her and she relented. As she left the room, she said: "If thou feels thissen going, blow yon candle out."

The farmer rallied; they continued with their miserably austere existence. One day they "lashed out" and bought a second-hand Land Rover. When the farmer died, he was so old a neighbour remarked: "I reckon t'Almighty must have forgitten him." His widow went to the local newspaper to put in "yan o' them death notices." The cost shocked her. The young man behind the counter said she could have the first six words for nothing. She wrote down: "Sam Dead. Land Rover for Sale."

A farmer's funeral is attended by a host of people clad in crow-black clothes. Farmers are very clannish and faithful to each other. There's plenty of talk, including speculation on how much the departed farmer has left. (That farmer spent the latter part of his life amassing money so his friends would be impressed when they read details of the will in the weekly paper). They do say that when a ninety-year-old man was leaving the churchyard after an interment, someone muttered: "There's not much point in him going home, is there?"

Aisgill, the highest point of the Settle-Carlisle, as it was
in Midland days. The signal box has been transferred to
a preserved railway in Derbyshire. Midland locomotives
are now museum pieces, but "steam specials" still rouse
the echoes in these high and normally lonely places. The
hill looming beyond the bridge is Wild Boar Fell. Local
becks form the nursery of the northward-running Eden,
which ripples through Mallerstang and into a fan-
shaped vale extending to the Scottish border.

The Railside Sheep of Ribblehead

THE ROYAL TRAIN, having stopped overnight at Dent, was on its way south with Queen Elizabeth (now the Queen Mother) on board. Men stationed by the bridges and at the ventilation shafts on Blea Moor kept a watchful eye on everyone who moved. Down at Ribblehead, half a dozen cows slipped through the cordon. They had been off-loaded from the evening pick-up train and were to spend the night penned at Ribblehead Station, awaiting collection by local farmers. Being ignorant cows, they had not read the railway manual. Instead of remaining quietly in the pens, they escaped and went foraging. Jack Towler, ganger, who was on Royal duty, told me with true Dales brevity and under-statement: "We got 'em back just afore she arrived."

Each September, the accent is on sheep. For the Ribblehead Sheep Show the best of the bunch are penned behind the *Station Inn*. These sheep are a distinctive breed, cheerfully tolerating the passage of trains at close range. Their territory is bisected by the Settle-Carlisle railway. George Horner, for years signalman at Blea Moor, has told me about the sheep which lived beside the tracks by the right of birth. A lot of 'em were lambed on t'tracks, being reared within yards of the clattering trains. If anyone tried to put a ewe off railway property, "t'owd devil would stand its ground, stamping its feet."

It was suggested that sheep should be provided with timetables. Someone with a sense of humour who compiled the special traffic notices forwarded a copy for the platelayers, another for the signalman and a third headed: "For the Attention of the Blea Moor Sheep". These animals have always been able to take care of themselves. A visiting inspector, standing in the signal box at Blea Moor, was perturbed to see a recumbent, cud-chewing sheep on the "four foot", where shortly an express train was due.

The inspector turned away in horror as the train rushed into view, but could not resist sneaking a glimpse, anxious to know the fate of the sheep. At the last moment it arose, stretched and walked off the track. George recalled: "Yon express shot by her at sixty miles an hour. Then she went back between t'rails and lay down again." When I last walked along the path beside the Blea Moor signal box, I saw a double fence system had been introduced, a deterrent to footloose ramblers and sheep.

James Taylor, who served as Stationmaster at Horton-in-Ribblesdale and Settle stations, used to negotiate with farmers about compensation for sheep which had strayed on to the railway and had died under the wheels of passing trains. He noticed that every dead sheep was "t'best in t'flock, Mr Taylor. Aye—it'd have browt a lot o' brass at t'sales." One farmer, finding a dead sheep on his land, heaved it over a wall on to the tracks, intending to put in a claim to the railway. He was startled when a passing (and unseen) permanent way man picked up the sheep and tossed it back!

Ribblehead, where a twenty-four arch railway viaduct has the visual emphasis of a row of exclamation marks, is a Mecca for walkers, potholers and (on prescribed days) for the photographers of "Steam Specials" using the Settle-Carlisle line. In good weather, Ingleborough and Whernside are in view and there's an ice cream van at the road junction.

In an area where the main road crosses stretches of open moor, sheep perish under the wheels of passing traffic. In spring, old motor tyres on posts carry white-painted notices: "Beware of Lambs". An American was heard to say: "Gee—they must be tough lambs which live in this area." The messages should be heeded. Lambs need time to attune themselves to traffic. The sheep are often nonchalent and, at times, they refuse to move from the centre of the road where they are excitedly licking the surface. Have they detected lingering traces of the rock-salt which was spread to de-ice the road in winter?

Ribblehead sheep are accustomed to weather extremes. After a burst of sunshine, the Weather Clerk stirs up a distinctive brand of cold, wet, windy weather. When Ribblehead had a Stationmaster, it was a much-valued weather station from which coded messages were sent to the Air Ministry for general distribution. The Stationmaster released a gas-filled balloon from the platform to assess the height of the cloud base. Rainfall details were requested, and the first year produced a figure in excess of 100 inches. The average annual rainfall is seventy inches.

Those who attend the Ribblehead Sheep Show would be wise to carry a raincoat. The weather is "variable". The Show is a revival of an old sheep sale held at the side of the approach road to Ribblehead station. The venue of the present Show, *The Station Inn,* has a gable-end reinforced against the Wet by sheets of corrugated iron. For twenty-six years, Joe Coates was "mine host" at the inn. Like many another publican in the Dales, he combined the task of drawing pints with stock-rearing, keeping a few cows and sheep. Joe's son, Keith, the current proprietor, took over in 1991.

The Ribblehead sheep are born, reared and spained, the ewes being separated from their lambs. A young and healthy breeding stock, wise to the ways of Ribblehead—the railway and the moors—is left to carry on the breed.

Deep Mid-Winter

There are places on these Pennine hills where the only sounds are the bleating of sheep or the tinkling of a mountain stream. This is solitude.

HJS (1965).

Just as it seemed that the hill farmer's lot was improving because of better lamb and calf prices, they have now been faced with cuts in payments made to compensate them for farming in the more difficult and less productive areas.

Robin Cradock, National Farmers' Union (1994).

If you want to stay in the Dales, you've got to accept a pitiful choice of jobs and pay.

Peter Annison, Hawes (1994).

Where the Snow Squeaks

DALESFOLK fear the east wind. The Helm Wind begins with an easterly draught of about fifteen miles an hour which cools in its ascent of the Pennines and eventually, in the vicinity of High Cup Nick, spills over into the Eden Valley, becoming turbulent as it meets and mixes with the warmer air. A wind rages along the East Fellside with such verocity, it is said to have "blawn t'nebs (beaks) off geese on t'green at Milburn." Rooks, scrounging twigs for their bulky nests, are reported to have been virtually blown into the valley—and to have walked back!

The Grandfather of Easterlies occurs, now and again, a few weeks after Christmas. When high pressure settles over the Continent and, to the south, the Alpine peaks stand out like monster ice-cream cornets against an azure sky, the wind running across the top of the high pressure system has an edge to it like Sheffield steel. Flurries of snow are seen at the Yorkshire Coast. On the Pennines—an east-west barrier to the weather systems—the snow is fine, crisp and stickable. So low has the temperature fallen by the upper Tees that the laid snow has squeaked underfoot. A Dales farmer, watching his sheep scutter to the lee of the walls, remarked grimly: "This'll mak t'owd yows bleat for a bit o' fodder."

Wintry showers from the south and west become snow-broth (slush) by teatime. A north-easterly blizzard outstays its welcome. It may arrive stealthily by night. Bill Alderson, of Angram, slept in a front bedroom overlooking upper Swaledale and facing east. He used to tell of t'neet when he was snawed-up i' bed. The weather was calm when he went to bed. As usual, he left his window open. Sleeping soundly, he did not hear sounds which indicated a strengthening wind, nor did he see the first hard, fine flurries of snow. Conditions were calm again when he awoke in the morning. He became aware that the bedroom was brighter than usual and then he realised that everything was powdery white with fresh snow—"all except where I was liggin; I'd thawed it oot." Bill shouted to his sister to open the door and then "loped straight oot o' bed into t'passage."

I know of few wilder places than the topmost reaches of Teesdale. At Cow Green, the climate in winter is sub-arctic, and over thirty-six degrees of frost have been recorded. During long periods of continuous frost, the river freezes over and in spring it bears jangling floes of ice. Tom Buffey, the site research officer when a dam was being built at Cow Green, lived in a caravan here for months, day and night. He became, unwittingly, an authority on the weather and told me of unexpected delights: "When there's a clear day, the early morning and evening are the most beautiful. The sun throws long shadows across the hags and vegetation; there's a variety of colouring—red, chestnut, brown, green, black—changing all the time. Add to this the shadows of fast-moving clouds and you do not have the same conditions for five minutes at a time."

Dalesfolk who lived through the wintry weather of February and March, 1947, shudder at the mere recollection of it. A normal fall of snow during January—and there is rarely much snow before Christmas—was followed early in February by a blizzard which continued relentlessy until the middle of March. Roadmen battled to open up the high roads by day and the wind filled them in again by night. On the updale farms, sheep were overblown and had to be dug out, the grazings were crusted over with snow and icy and the hay crop which had been light and of "very moderate stuff" was used up before the arrival of a tardy spring.

The farmers went through the ritual of milking cattle with little chance of getting the milk away on the lorries of the Milk

Marketing Board, the establishment of which in the 1930s had ended the traditional butter-making. There was no way of preserving the milk, which had to be fed back to the cattle or poured down the drains. The farmer's wife, beset by rationing so soon after the war, had not been able to lay in a large stock of food and fuel.

In Swaledale, where wave-like drifts of snow rose to telegraph-post height in places, the snow-clearers included German prisoners of war and soldiers from Catterick Camp. Above Thwaite, the dale was cut off. Dick Guy, taking a load of hay to one of the high farms on March 12, as yet another blizzard stirred itself, was soon stuck in snow. The lorry could not be moved for nine days. A district nurse, summoned to Black How Farm, Ravenseat, one of the topmost farms, where a baby was expected, drove her car to Thwaite, walked to Keld and travelled on ponyback—with a police escort!—to the farm, where the baby was delivered with little time to spare. The District Nurse, summoned to Angram during the same grim spell of weather, plodded from Thwaite, with military escort, fore and aft. On yet another snowbound journey, to Whaw in Arkengarthdale, she covered the last stretch sitting on a horse-drawn sledge.

At Capna (Capon Hall), on Malham Moor, in that never-to-be-forgotten winter, the Carr family looked out on ''a vast whiteness''. Soon the household food was running out and hardly any of the cattle food remained. Edith Carr recalls: ''The cattle were 'bawling' all day. We could not feed them too much at a time and they were permanently hungry. Every evening, the sky was blood-red. There would be more frost or snow. All was engulfed.''

When the storm abated, Robert Carr, swaddled in normal clothes, plus greatcoat, scarf and cap, set off on horseback to get some food. He returned at dusk with some potatoes and porridge oats, tied to the horse's back. Another time, a German prisoner of war who had been helping at the farm took the horse down to Settle for food. He was away for so long that the Carrs were uneasy, then alarmed when the horse returned without its rider. Robert went in search of him. The German was found lying in the snow and it was only the movement of an arm that had attracted attention to him. "Next day," Edith recalled, "we could trace his wavering journey back to the farm by the bits and pieces of groceries he had dropped on the snow."

In that wintry spell, Edith broke her arm. And one of the roadmen was killed. He had been working with the snow plough and had the misfortune to stumble and fall in front of it. The body was borne to Capna and laid out in the front room where the Carr children, detecting something unusual, began to wail. There was high drama as the RAF dropped some fodder for the starving stock. As they listened to the radio, the Carr family heard their farm mentioned along with others as places due for a mercy-flight with fodder for the stock.

Edith recalls: "In the morning, we made a large cross of sacks laid on the frozen snow. We waited and listened. About 3 p.m., we could hear planes approaching. Dakotas swooped down low over the farm buildings, dropping their precious cargo in the meadows...We plunged through the snow towards the hay bales. All had burst open. Hay was squandered about. We struggled in deep snow till night, dragging the hay inside, then feeding the cattle."

By April, when conditions ameliorated, half the stock had died. Edith showed me the croft in which 22 cows were buried. That patch of ground had long since returned to its normal appearance. Some highly vocal geese were its only inhabitants...

At Home with a Dales Historian

HOME CROFT, at Linton-in-Craven, was the home for over fifty years of Arthur Raistrick, the Dales historian and pioneer of industrial archaeology. Arthur died in 1991, at the age of ninety-four. I corresponded with him for many years, subbed many of the articles he wrote for *The Dalesman* and occasionally, on impulse, called to see him.

I was never likely to catch Arthur Raistrick in bed in the morning. He always rose early and spent the first hour listening to classical music played on his old gramophone. Then he settled down, in a ten feet square study, which was so crowded there was no space for a door to swing. A double curtain cut off the study from the hall.

Once or twice, as I crossed the threshhold of Home Croft, my nostrils told me it was baking day. His wife, Elizabeth—herself no mean writer and historian—chatted with me in the kitchen, after providing me with coffee and fresh-baked scones. She had a fund of good Yorkshire stories and told me of a funeral procession which was passing up Skipton High Street. A well-dressed and somewhat arrogant lady visitor pushed her way through to the front of the gathering of spectators and asked, in a superior voice: "Who is dead?" A dalesman replied: "Him in't box, missis."

Arthur's contribution was food for the mind. He would invite me into the main living room (formerly the mewstead of the barn) to inspect documents and illustrations connected with his latest research. One day, every level surface was covered with old lead-mining photographs which he was assembling for an important picture book on the industry. We never discussed food. Arthur was finicky about what he ate though once, having met him and several others for a discussion on industrial archaeology, I repaired to a Skipton restaurant and found him tucking in to deep fried haddock and chips.

I never left Home Croft without having been stimulated, in some research I was doing, by ideas thrown across to me by Arthur Raistrick. He did not provide answers; he suggested courses of inquiry. Once we discussed the name Wild Boar Fell. I thought it sounded too romantic to have been used by the Norse folk. Arthur mentioned the inevitable confusion over recording placenames when an Ordnance Survey party from the South Country met some untutored countryfolk in rural Westmorland. I told him of my research into the Hoffman Kiln, at the Craven Quarry, Langcliffe, and how I thought the process of continous lime-burning had worked. Arthur recalled (unbraggingly) that in the 1930s when he had taken a party of university students to see it, the Kiln was actually being operated!

Arthur was born at Saltaire in 1896. When I told him that on my journey up the dale I had been humming "Deep Harmony", a famous West Riding hymn tune, he mentioned that as a lad he met the composer, Handel Parker. One of Arthur's uncles was a member of the hymn-writer's male voice choir. He called at the Raistrick home and said: "You must come along to our rehearsal, lad. Mr Parker's trying out a new hymn tune on us!"

Arthur was fond of talking about his family connections with the Dales. Charles Raistrick, his great grandfather, had been a well-known cattle dealer—and a skilful poacher. He was one one of the men who introduced the small Irish cattle into the area, collecting them after they had been landed at Liverpool. Arthur had been taken to the Dales as a babe in arms. He could remember every worth-while Dales experience from the age of six.

The earliest Raistrick letter in my archives is a copy of one written to *The Yorkshire Dalesman* magazine in 1940. Arthur mentioned he had decided to give up his Readership at University College, Newcastle-on-Tyne, for the duration of the war. He and his wife would be experimenting with simple living. He might even purchase a bicycle for increased mobility.

It was Elizabeth who told me about their scheme for barn conversion which took place in 1940. When the building was bought, and plans were drawn-up to convert it, they had found it to be almost devoid of right angles. Elizabeth and Arthur settled down in their beloved Wharfedale with an Aga cooker, a boiler for radiators "and as much electrical equipment as we could afford—vacuum cleaner, washer and refrigerator". It was an impressive list considering these items were bought at the beginning of the last war. They also acquired a wide view, extending from Greenhow and Fancarl Crag, round past Elbolton and other reef knolls to the line of Thorpe Fell.

Arthur had no car; he walked or used public transport where possible. When I parked my car at Linton, I usually did so out of sight of the house! Arthur had many good friends who gave him a lift in their cars if he wished to re-visit the remoter parts of the Dales. He was conveyed by car up the steep hill from Threshfield to the moor-edge when an excavation was taking place at a former colliery. That day, though he was an old man, Arthur stood for an hour or two in cold and damp. His handsome face was now somewhat shrunken and seamed, his fine grey hair windblown, and he looked for all the world like an Old Testament prophet. Someone had described him as being "like a piece of his own rugged mountain limestone."

He was the author of over 39 books and 150 pamphlets and papers. To me, Arthur Raistrick was as well-known for his don'ts as his do's. He did not hesitate to write about mistakes in the magazine. I got a waspish letter from him when we published our first (and only) cigarette advertisement. When I took a tape-recorder to Home Croft, he refused to talk into it and subsequently sent me a two-page letter urging me not to rely on tapes. Such interviews had been proved (scientifically) to be unreliable.

When he was ninety years old, I contacted some of his close friends, including "the gang" (a group of women who met at his home once a week for talk and tea). Their eulogies were published as a birthday tribute in *The Dalesman*. He warmly acknowledged the gift of a copy of the magazine. I was pleased to note that "I have long counted you among my close friends". He signed the letter "Arthur".

The Art of Reginald Smith

THE MOST successful of the Dales landscape painters, using the great outdoors as their studio, have the ability to work quickly in water-colours. Weather systems succeed each other with a bewildering speed and it-may be sunny on one side of the dale and raining on the other. Fred Lawson, setting off on foot, and having to paint or sketch when his energy ran out, had often got no further than "the scraggy edges of the moors, where there's a few trees." There, under a greyish sky, he began to paint. Constance Pearson, working in Malhamdale, might return home with a rain-spattered painting. She had achieved spontaneity, which is the hall-mark of good water-colouring.

Arthur Reginald Smith painted his beloved Wharfedale, invariably out of doors, having first made a charcoal sketch which he simplified until just the bare bones of the landscape were revealed. His best-known Dales pictures are of the valley at dawn or late afternoon. He studied the tree-shaded trout pools of the Wharfe itself. He enjoyed making snow studies and in very cold weather added some whisky to his painting water.

When in his prime as a painter, Arthur Reginald Smith did not stand out in a crowd. A photograph taken for the *Yorkshire Observer* at an important London exhibition in 1934 shows his unprepossessing appearance in profile. He had a reasonably sturdy figure but was balding and peered somewhat shyly through thin-framed spectacles. Was it nonchalence or nervousness which made him put his hands in his trouser pockets? One who knew him well referred to the "plain manliness" of his appearance. Reggie Smith (as he was known to his special friends) was "quietly reserved and did not advertise his occupation."

He commanded the attention of London critics because the Princess of Wales showed interest in his work and had commissioned paintings of interiors at Marlborough House. A contemporary newspaper report of his 1934 exhibition was headed "Yorkshire Grandeur" and sub-titled "Clever Work of Skipton Artist". The writer mentioned the "happy chance" which led to the artist being born at Skipton, the "gateway to the Yorkshire Dales", for he "takes a delight in Northern grandeur as against the mere prettiness so often found in the South...He interprets scenes of dale and fell...with the understanding of the Yorkshire born."

My interest in Reginald Smith began with a browse through Halliwell Sutcliffe's book *The Striding Dales*, for which Smith provided a dozen water-colours and a selection of line drawings. The book was published by Warne in 1929 as an edition of 250 copies (at a retail price of 30s). A second edition appeared in 1933. I could not remember the book's launch, being only a year old at the time, but M'duke Miller, mine host of *The Falcon* at Arncliffe (and a well-known water-colourist), whom I met periodically, was sure to mention Reginald Smith's work.

The author Halliwell Sutcliffe lived at White Abbey, Linton-in-Craven. *The Striding Dales* followed a string of unmemorable novels and made his name. The dalesfolk were accustomed to seeing the tall, aesthetic-looking Sutcliffe tramping about the district, wearing shirt and shorts, and by the mid-1930s almost every house in Wharfedale had a copy of his book, with its jaunty, romantic—and not always accurate—impressions of Dales life, lore and history. The illustrations which Warne, the publishers, had commissioned for the book helped to popularise the work of Reginald Smith, who was then living at Threshfield, a mile or two from Sutcliffe's home.

Reginald Smith, born at Skipton in 1873, was a chemist's son but had farming relatives. From an early age, art appealed to him. His parents felt that teaching was a more dependable career, but in the end it was art that triumphed. He studied art and then taught it at Keighley. He practised art (with the help of scholarships) in Italy and other parts of Europe. It is related that when in Italy he lost his nerve, having crossed the precipitous head of a ravine, he sat down, unpacked his tackle and made a sketch, which put him in a calmer frame of mind so that he could get away from his perilous circumstance—on hands and knees!

Reginald Smith's work was exhibited at the Royal Academy and through The Royal Watercolour Society, of which (in 1914) he became an associate. As related, his work came to the attention of the Princess of Wales (later Queen Mary) who later invited him to paint interiors at Buckingham Palace. His best-known period dates from the outbreak of the 1914-18 war, when (as the number of art students dwindled and London became vulnerable to enemy action) he moved his family—his wife, the former Miss Petty of Sutton, his son and two daughters—from London to Threshfield, where he built a new studio.

At first he felt cut-off from the centre of the art world, but then he discovered that mid-Wharfedale held a coterie of talented men, including the artists Reginald Brundrit and John Smith Atherton. Though Reginald Smith considered that art was a full-time job, he did manage to join a group which met to read Shakespeare and occasionally he was to be seen in the small choir at Linton church.

In summer, Reginald Smith painted, mainly out-of-doors. In winter, he settled down happily to produce charming line drawings, such as those to be found in *The Striding Dales*. J Keighley Snowden, a friend who lived at Steeton and made a mark though his imaginative photography, recalled Smith's runabout car, "with the easel on the back seat", a car which was "known to early-rising shepherds in winter." He regarded all his work with a censorious eye, eliminating and simplifying, and told his wife: "When I'm satisfied, it'll be a bad sign."

In course of time, he captured every nuance of Wharfedale and its river. Humphrey Brooke, a Yorkshireman who was secretary of the Royal Academy for seventeen years until 1968, wrote, with Reginald Smith in mind: "The Wharfe is the only river I know which has had its own poet in paint". Brooke added: "For the most part, his attention was concentrated in an area of about thirty square miles around his home."

Fred Allen, a nonagenarian Keighlian, now living in the Dales, showed me paintings by Reginald Smith dating from boyhood—the earliest, when he was fourteen years old. Already the artist was showing an awareness of time and season, which became the hallmark of his finest work. T C Butterfield, principal of Keighley School of Art at the time when Reginald Smith was on the staff, was to recall how the young artist would be out of bed bright and early. He would bring with him to School "morning effects painted at Skipton—often canal scenes with the church tower, the woods or the castle..."

This special talent for immediacy in his work is seen in an early springtime study of trees, which is not just a commentary on the obvious. Reginald Smith saw the hint of green about trees which would soon burst into leaf. His sheep were not just sheep but heavily pregnant yows. Rooks were portrayed as they poked about among the remains of last year's nests which they would soon be renovating. A brooding moorscape look devoid of life until you noticed two sheep, as inconspicuous as boulders but included in the picture because they were there by the right of a thousand generations. I have seen the original of a pastoral study, "Miss Hugill's Caravan". This was one of the horse-drawn variety and belonged to Miss Hugill, art mistress at Keighley Grammar School in about 1917.

I have pondered on many of Reginald Smith's distinctive grey-green paintings of Wharfedale, and particularly of his beloved River Wharfe around Bolton Priory, where it has a park-like setting. Sir Charles Holmes sagely wrote that the artist's dominant mood was "a gentle austerity, corresponding to the county he loved best." The word "mood" is appropriate to almost all his work. Reginald Smith's watercolours express mood, season and time of day. He kept unsociable hours, lugging his painting equipment to selected viewpoints to record the effect of light on landscape at dusk or early morning. He told John Marsh in 1927 (two years before the publication of the first edition of *The Striding Dales*): "There is a certain tranquil beauty about the day when the sun is rising, something quietly lovely about the hills and river when the world is half asleep..."

When an exhibition was held at Bradford in 1979, the introductory notes referred to "these shimmering scenes of dawn and dusk" which were painted with a limited palette of colours. "Broad but delicate effects were achieved by using a large brush which dragged the pigment over the paper, leaving isolated pinpricks of uncovered ground that gave sparkle and vitality to all parts of the picture. The initial structure of the composition would be summarily but firmly indicated in charcoal."

J Keighley Snowden recalled how Reginald Smith stood on cork mats in the snow. "Wind was his only enemy," he wrote. "All weathers else, morning and evening, autumn, winter and spring, were welcome allies of an absorbing passion..." Like many landscape painters, he was overwhelmed by the thousand shades of green in summer, preferring the "sober browns and greys" of winter and early spring. An art critic of the 1930s, commenting on the painting "Summer in Langstroth Dale", wrote of the artist's use of delicate colouring "as if he feared the brilliant grass and trees of the valleys...this picture lacks the strength of his other works."

His happiness with the Dales landscape was matched by the pleasure he derived from visits to the Lake District, having been commissioned by Warne to provide a series of paintings for W G Collingwood's *The Lake Counties* (a work uniform with *The Striding Dales).* In an exhibition which featured "Behind the Dunes—Prestatyn" it was his sombre "Mardale—Evening" which caught the eye of a critic, who wrote with elation of Smith's treatment of a dark hill which "towers up into the heavens." Reginald Smith was a dedicated man who worked on broadly traditional lines, abhoring the modernism which was creeping in. He referred to "stunts to catch the silly public" and "tricks to evade drawing."

Fred Allen, himself a keen amateur artist, showed me his collection of framed prints—pictures used in *The Striding Dales*—which had come to him from Smith's relations, the Irving family of Skipton. The artist stayed overnight with the Irvings when he intended to catch the early morning train to London. The most northerly Smith painting is surely that owned by a Littondale-born man who has lived for years at Reykjavik, in Iceland.

At the age of sixty-two, Reginald Smith was drowned at the Strid, where the Wharfe swirls and bubbles in a narrow channel between banks of gritstone. Some of his equipment was found on one bank and other items were picked up on the other bank. Had he unwisely responded to the challenge of leaping across the Strid, only to slip back into the water? Or was there a more ominous reason for his death?

His friend, J Keighley Snowden, wrote: "The wild stream had taken his life, and that gesture was fitting to a fine modesty. It marked his devotion to a beautiful English dale, where the best of his work had been done very happily; and it was not theatrical but in quiet keeping with the sincerity of that work, which never allowed a pose or a spectacular effect."

His will decreed that his ashes should be consigned to the river. The place chosen was Yockenthwaite, within a mile or so of where two mountain becks join to form the River Wharfe...

Photographing the Dales Parrot

THE NEAREST I came to being sea-sick in the Dales was when Stan, a naturalist friend, found the nest of a pair of green woodpeckers in some semi-natural woodland near Hubberholme. Having obtained permission to photograph the birds, he set about making a pylon-hide, using old wood from a cottage being renovated at Buckden. The hide culminated in a platform on which he erected a tent of wood and hessian.

Two holes were made so that he and his camera might look directly at the nesting hole. Stan, ever-generous, invited me to have a photographic session. He hoped the birds would not attack the woodwork because "it's full of woodworm". And he hoped I would not feel queazy as the structure swayed under my weight and the breeze.

Apart from the gentle swaying of the hide, and the occasional stomach-flutter, it was a magical evening. The woodland was banded with yellow sunlight. A shaft of light fell directly on the nesting hole. When the green, yellow and red woodpecker arrived with food for its young, there was a touch of Oriental splendour. A green woodpecker looks stocky and gaudy—the Dales equivalent of a parrot. A green body is off-set by a patch of yellow at the rump and red features on its crown. Though shy, this woodpecker has a laughing call which resounds in areas where trees are thinly spread.

At the wood above Hubberholme, the young woodpeckers, with chirring hunger-calls, stuck their heads from the nesting hole. Feeding time was at hourly intervals. Meanwhile, I absorbed the sights and sounds of a tract of semi-natural woodland of a type which, all over the Dales, dons an autumnal coat of many colours.

Some of the fine old woods of the Dales are dying and might be lost for ever. A recent survey has revealed overgrazing by livestock, leading to a decline in the number of indigenous trees. Sheep in particular are avid grazers, shearing off any plant material which pops its head above the ground. Bracken, also the alien beech and sycamore, are encroaching. So concerned is the new Forestry Authority that the owners of semi-natural woodland throughout the land are being offered £80 compensation for every hectare they are prepared to fence off. Hopefully, this will be done for up to ten years so these areas will regenerate naturally.

A wood never sleeps. At what dalesfolk call "the edge o' dark", the badger's striped head is seen at the mouth of its sett as it tastes the air. If the tang of human scent is detectable, the badger will stay below ground. In my badger-watching days, I sat on a branch, about twelve feet above the ground, for the hour before dark when badgers at the remoter Dales setts begin to stir.

In spring, the woodcock goes by, some fifty feet above the ground, its wings beating slowly, its head jerking backwards as it utters sounds which Paul Holmes, first warden at Malham Tarn Field Centre, once described to me as "three grunts and a squeak". The woodcock was "roding", circling its territory. Down below was the nest, the eggs cushioned on oak leaves and the female woodcock, splendidly camouflaged, sitting her eggs so tightly she might be detected only by a sparkle in her eye.

May is a good time for both badger and woodcock watching. The badger cubs, on receiving the "all clear", romp into view and play noisy games in the bracken. An autumn delight is watching an adult badger taking fresh bedding into the sett, trapping bundles of dead bracken between forelegs and chin as it slithers backwards. In autumn, the old tracts of woodland are in carnival mood. Freeholders' Wood, in

Wensleydale, has a management scheme to ensure it has a future as well as a fascinating past. In Grass Wood, Wharfedale, trees stand with arms full of tinted leaves and "fungus forays" are held.

Woodland on Giggleswick Scar, which is seen by pleasure motorists who are taking a sentimental trip up Buckhaw Brow following the diversion of the A65, is to be returned to its original structure. A population of native species of trees will be given conditions in which they will perpetuate themselves naturally. Gone from Giggleswick Scar is a deathly blanket of larch, which looks bright and cheerful when leafing up in spring but becomes dark and dense at other times of the year.

William Wordsworth, writing about the introduction of new commercial strains to the Lake District at the time of the Industrial Revolution, called the new larch plantations "vegetable manufactury". The Poet, who knew Wharfedale well, commended the way the Strid Woods had been opened out by the creation of a system of paths and vantage points. Wordsworth was one of the Romantic Age visitors to the Dales who noticed goats romping on the crags. One group was to be found around Malham Cove and another in the area of Kilnsey Crag.

Goats are adroit, placing their feet on the trunk of a tree to reach up and produce a high browse line. They "eit all afore 'em", going through a wood like the proverbial dose of salts.

Artful Dodgers on the Skyline

A FARMER'S SON was driving cows through Horton-in-Ribblesdale when he was asked: "Are you Harry Morphet's son?" The cowherd nodded. "I thought so...I ken thee dog." Farming in the Dales depends on sheepdogs—the Artful Dodgers on the skyline. The best dogs are seen pitting their wits against sheep on the trials grounds in their own television programme—*One Man and his Dog*.

The handler gives a series of cool, clear whistles—a sort of canine morse code—and evokes immediate reactions from the dog. Go left! Go right! Stop! Come on! The traditional commands are simple, unemotional. A group of Swaledale sheep, straight off t'fell, is persuaded to take an unsheep-like course between hurdles, round a post, into a pen. The task occupies eight or nine minutes and (says a supporter) you can take more out of a dog in that short time than if you'd been working it on t'fells for hours.

Adrian Bancroft, one of the long-time members of the Yorkshire Sheepdog Society, thinks that excitement helps. So he puts "a little tension" on the dog during a trial. This falls short of what happened in a strange drive at Northallerton (recalled by Sam Dyson, a judge) when some big heavy sheep were released. Two of them dropped dead within minutes, leaving the dog-handler with only one sheep to pen.

Though the average price of a good dog is £500, the very best animals command over twice that figure—and are worth it. A well-trained dog makes it possible for a farmer to run sheep over tracts of hill-country with the assurance that he may gather then quickly for routine farm operations—dipping, clipping—or the onset of snow. James Hogg, the Ettrick Shepherd (1770-1835) wrote of the sheepdog:

"Without him, the mountainous land in England and Scotland would not be worth sixpence. It would require more hands to manage a flock of sheep, gather them from the hills, force them into...folds and drive them to market than the profit of the whole is capable of maintaining."

Charles Scott, writing of a working collie in Scotland a century ago, created a word picture which might apply to the Dales today: "The shepherd addresses a few words to his dog, which darts off like a greyhound. We watch him spanking across the glen, now clearing a wide ditch at a bound, then fording a stream, half wading, half swimming. He waits but for a moment to shake the water from his coat. His master calls to him. He raises his head and ears to listen to the order which is repeated...He now comes in sight of the sheep, and in getting ahead of them takes a wide, circular course."

Dales farmers do not glamorise their dogs. Said a man I met at a sheepdog trial: "They're all curs really. We christen 'em Border Collies". Each has a short, sharp name—Meg, Beth, Floss, Tim—which has carrying power on being shouted out-of-doors. Man has developed the dog's aptitude for gathering sheep. Some animals show promise at three months, but "there's a difference in dogs. Old Nell, a black and tan, was the best moor dog I ever had—and she never looked at a sheep till she was two years old." A dog which was "worth nowt" was heard being commanded by its master to: "Come back wi' thee. I'll do t'job missen."

The television series, *One Man and his Dog*, is shot in areas of splendid scenery, which adds to the appeal. Many a trial associated with a Dales agricultural show—such as at Muker, in Swaledale—appeals to urban visitors because, on a sunlit day, the showfield, fells, woods and sky glow like a setting for grand opera. It's a sport in which the dog rather than the handler tends to be the star. The regular trial grounds are well-known by name. At Hawes, for the past nine years, the best north-country trialists have met for a trial associated in name with the late Len Prince. It commemorates a well-known dog-trainer who died tragically when hit by a falling tree and profits from the trial go to local charities.

The sheep which a collie dog has to match its wits against are selected with care. Animals fresh from the fells would be too frisky by far. The competitors must also have the assurance that the sheep have been inspected and are basically sound and with an even temperament. On the trials ground, faced with sheep, hurdles, judges and a clock, the successful dog is one which responds most surely to the whistles of command from its master; it must not crowd nor scare the sheep; and it would be penalised if it barked.

In farm conditions, barking rouses those sheep which languish out of sight in a mini-jungle of bracken. When a North Craven farmer, Jimmy Wilson told his dogs to speak, they had to bark! Handler and dog act like one towards a given object—penning the sheep. It is a collaboration which has almost a mystical quality. At gathering time, when sheep from half a fell are collected by half a dozen farmers and as many, if not more, dogs, the effect can be spectacular as over a ridge comes a tightly-packed flock of sheep—a mass of animals, spilling down the fellside like a grey lava flow.

Curiously, it's the daft dog which often works best when sheep have been overblown by snow and the farmer is anxious to find them before they are smothered. Sheep, giving way before a blizzard, find sheltered places where they can go no further; here they stay, while the snow continues to fall. If the snow is crisp, the sheep find themselves in snow caves created by the warmth of their bodies. The rising warmth creates a small air-hole, with brownish edges, which is not easy to find.

I asked Bill Alderson, of Swaledale, how he had found overblown sheep. He smiled and replied: "I've fun 'em all sorts of ways—sometimes deeard!" Bill and others prodded drifts with rake shafts, indicating where sheep were lying or perhaps opening up an air passage from which scent could spread to a dog with a good nose. "A dog 'at's used to it walks at t'wind side so it gets t'scent." One sheep lay in a drift for five days and came out wick (alive).

A sheepdog is at its peak of efficiency at five years old. Those dogs which have performed well are pensioned off; they spend their latter days sleeping on t'flags in t'farmyard and have a cosy kennel for the night. Do Pennine collies chase sheep in their dreams?

Their successors are now regarded more as partners than canine servants. Sam Dyson, of Stanbury, says: "The best type o' dog is one that'll stand straightening up (correcting) and yet, when you've finished with it, is still pals with you. If it starts to sulk or owt like that, you get nowhere." When Sam wants to contact his wife, Peggy, in a crowded supermarket, he gives a selection of his trial-ground whistles.

Hearing about this practice, a woman said to Peggy: "He wouldn't whistle at me, you know." Said Peggy: "He would—if he'd lived with you for fifty years!"

A Dales Christmas

CHRISTMAS began with a goose—more precisely, with the promise of a goose, the major prize in the annual whist drive. Every village had its Christmas whist, which was packed, regardless of the weather. Outside, the Weather Clerk sprinkled some snow on the fells. Inside, it was warm enough, but there was a chilliness at the tables. The play was intense. Revoke, when playing a card, at your peril...

An old farmer, holding out a hand as broad as a door and rough as sandpaper unsmilingly invited you to "cut the pack". The quartet of ladies from the market town, who never missed a Christmas whist drive, infiltrated the company and played humourlessly. There was nowt funny about t'Christmas whist drive, with a Christmas dinner at stake.

The evening snack was something better than the two sandwiches, biscuit and cake of normal social evenings. It was, of course, a Jacob's Join "do", with everyone contributing. How Jacob got in on the act had long been forgotten. The oldest folk remembered when t'Methodists called it a faith supper. Then someone remarked: "I've more faith than t'lot of you; I've browt nowt." Clearly, a change of name was needed. Generosity was a keynote of the Jacob's Join. Everyone might eat his or her fill. There was a special way to tackle it for maximum gain. Sit down early and chew each morsel slowly and well so "thou doesn't fill thissen wi' wind".

At a Dales farm, where work was continuous, regardless of the day, there was not much fuss at Christmas. Men with blackened faces and fancy costumes used to tour parts of the upper dales, knocking on doors and then entering to sing.

Of course, they expected some form of payment—cash or kind. On Christmas morning, the local brass band went busking, invariably—in the old sequence of cold winters—with snow lying deep and crisp and even. The bandsmen became increasingly unsteady as they were offered drinks which were a little stronger than lemonade.

Christmas decorations in a farm or cottage were usually restricted to a few bits of greenery, placed on window cills or hung from one of the hooks set in the kitchen ceiling. A Wensleydale man recalls: "On Christmas Day, we had oranges and apples and a few tinselly things. Nowt expensive. One year we had a few nuts and a sugar-pig." Christmas feasting included a roast of pork and some boiled ham, with plum pudding. But the centrepiece of the Christmas board was goose, not turkey.

Lots of people fattened geese for Christmas. A good goose laid its eggs on or about Old Candlemas Day (February 14) but in the high dale country the date was usually about February 20. At Sedbusk, in Wensleydale, Tom Thwaite had geese trailing about t'village. He kept his sitting birds in tea chests, set on their sides, each chest having a piece of zinc in front of the hole to restrain the bird. He kept the goslings for a month or two and sold them to men from the ploughing areas, who fattened them up on the stubble.

When Swaledale goslings were a month old, some of them were taken with the adult birds to the moor. Geese on Stonesdale Moor were gathered in the autumn and, herded by a dog, were driven to Muker. On the following day, they continued their journey over the moors to Askrigg station, where they were consigned by train to their new owners. The demand for geese was met by farmers over a wide area. Settle had its goose fair. The birds had been driven into town, some of them having first been directed through pools of tar to reinforce their webbed feet against the roughness of the road.

Geese kept at home were "crammed" with oatmeal or grain just before Christmas, for—as everyone should know—

a green goose (one reared on grass alone) was "nea gooid". A knife to the back of the head was the customary way of despatching a goose. Neighbours might call just before Christmas to help with the plucking. Some folk removed the feathers by scalding; elsewhere, they were plucked in a dry state. The Swinglehursts of Keasden singed the goose carcasses with a blowlamp before washing them.

A mixture of goose blood and oatmeal was prepared as puddings. Goose grease was kept for sore throats. There had to be a jar of grease for "raw chests" or bad coughs in winter. Goose-down was stuffed into a bag, which was placed in the oven, drying out the down and, hopefully, destroying parasites. Goose-wings were kept to be used at spring-cleaning time. They were ideal for removing cobwebs from behind large pieces of furniture.

At a farm on Malham Moor, forty years ago, one Christmas Day dawned without evidence of the special nature of the day. The children demanded a Christmas tree so mother led some of them across the Moor, which was bound hard by snow and frost and they eventually took a conifer from a plantation. The tree was borne triumphantly home and set up in a tub in the living room. The farmer's wife then went off to hand-milk the few cows. One of the children rushed into the shippon to report that the Christmas tree had caught fire. Frantically, mother made for the house, only to be told the fire had been put out—by throwing over it milk from a large jug! That Christmas, the cloying smell of burnt milk hung heavily in the rooms of the farmhouse.

Dalesfolk were not a fanciful people but those who felt moved by the Christmas atmosphere made a point of visiting the "coo byre" on the eve of St Stephen's Day (December 26) in the hope of seeing the cows kneel in their stalls in commemoration of the saint's martyrdom.

T'Owd Man's Domain

MUCH HAS been written about the lead-mines of the northern dales. In Upper Swaledale and Arkengarthdale, where mining lead was for centuries a thriving industry, the names of the mines remind us of people and places: Sir George, Priscilla, Dolly; Blakethwaite, Brandy Bottle Plane and Old Gang. Collections of lead-mining equipment are to be found at Hawes, Reeth, Earby and elsewhere.

What are now desolate little gills, frequented by sheep and ramblers, once bustled with human activity. A visitor to Gunnerside Gill, as an example, would see horse-drawn tubs loaded with galena (lead ore) rumbling from underground workings and hear the creaking of the big wooden wheels at the dressing-floors and the clang of a blacksmith's hammer as he sharpened the jumper-bars by which holes were driven in solid rock. The spring sandwort, a lead-tolerant plant, produces its white starry flowers in areas which t'Owd Man disturbed.

T'Owd Man is a collective term for generations of men who wrested a living by mining the fickle veins of lead. The mining community consisted of large families who fed themselves on smallholdings and otherwise subsisted on what they made while backing their hunches in the orefield. The miners were proud men who enjoyed their work. Many were freelances who, one day, would assuredly strike it rich!

In winter, a miner scarcely saw the daylight. He went underground while it was yet dark and returned home after sunset. Most times of the year, a surface worker at the mines did not need a watch; he could tell the time by relating the position of the sun to the edge of the deep gill in which the mines were set. The mining country might be powdered white with snow, and the entrances to the adits draped with icicles, but underground the temperature was pleasantly mild.

A typical miner's home, as described to me forty years ago by Robert Gill of Reeth, was small and primitive, often attached to a small-holding, so that the miner—before setting off for work—would milk and fodder a few cows. He left the rest of the farm work to his wife. The house sparkled with housewiferly pride. Steel fire-irons and fender, shining like silver, contrasted with the jet black of the oven door and the side boiler. Running almost the full width of the room, a foot or so below the ceiling, was the stannock, a piece of wood on which a jumble of clothes was airing. Always there were clothes to dry.

Breakfast for a miner consisted of thick porridge, salty bacon and good, strong tea. The food packed up for consumption at mid-day was plain but wholesome—wheatcake, sarfey (cheese, to be roasted over a candle flame), soda cake (a form of scone) and, as an occasional treat, prune pie. The stones of prunes littered some of the workings. Cold tea was carried in a tin bottle. The miner was ready to set off for work at seven o'clock. He wore a coarse shirt, moleskin jacket (with a large leather button from which to hang a couple of candles) and tight-fitting trousers to reduce drag in the workings.

A miner heading for work usually had good company. Many a pair of clogs rang on the metalled roads and took on a dull clumping sound as they negotiated the old trods of the gillside. Here and there, the miners rested for sufficient time to allow anyone who wished to smoke, using black twist in a clay pipe. The men usually rested in a squatting posture and they chatted about— mining. Now and again, some workings were sketched on the moist path with a stick to illustrate a point of discussion.

Arrival at an adit or mine-shaft was not the end of the

journey. There might be a half mile walk-cum-crawl for one or two men who had arranged a monthly bargain for getting lead with the agent for the mine. They would be paid on the quantity of ore brought out— after it had been washed. They worked by the light of long tallow candles which were attached to the walls of the mine with gobbets of clay.

They drilled with a jumper (iron bar) and hammer. The man who held the bar against the rock turned it slightly after it had been struck. When a hole had been drilled, a stick of gelignite was packed inside and wadded. A candle flame was applied to the fuse. The men retreated. When the explosion came and the rock face was shattered, the men eagerly looked among the rubble for pieces of galena. The oldest miners remembered when rock was shattered using unslagged lime. Then came black powder. Gelignite was noisy but efficient.

The dense atmosphere of the mine led to ill-health and premature death for dozens of miners. A gruver (the name given to lead miners, particularly those who worked underground) might suffer from lead-poisoning or silicosis, from inhaling dusty air. The local graveyards were half full of the bodies of miners who died in their fifties.

Returning home, a miner usually had a cooked meal, with potatoes and turnips. Even then, mining was not forgotten. It was obsessive. Men crowded into one of the living rooms, where smoke from the fire merged with smoke from their clay pipes, and they talked until the striking clock ushered them to their homes—and to bed.

Old Gang, in a side valley between Swaledale and Arkengarthdale, is a place where the days of t'Owd Man are easily evoked with reference to the remains of an early nineteenth century smelt mill and well preserved chimney. A large flue extended, as straight as a broomshaft, to Healaugh Crag, half a mile away. Here a chimney was built. Noxious fumes killed off the vegetation for many yards round about.

At the moor-edge at Old Gang are the gable-ends and stone pillars of what used to be an impressively long, thatched peat-house, where the drying process begun on the moor might continue, the peat-house being open to any drying winds though protected from rain. The "peeat pots" are traceable on the moor, though silting-up has taken place. Some of them would originally be five feet deep.

Visiting Old Gang with Matthew Cherry, I heard of the days when, as a lad, he had been accompanied by his grandfather, Annas Bill (his real name was Bill Buxton). The big mines were on their way out as early as the 1870s. Grandfather, who with some cronies spent his weekdays taking lead ore from the Dam Level and dressing it for delivery by horse and cart to the railway station at Richmond, told of the unquenchable faith of a miner in his ability to find lead, and of the times when galena was found in abundance and cunningly concealed by clay so that just enough was brought out of a level to keep up the price fixed with the agent.

Some miners attained old age. They were prospectors to the last. One veteran, who was said to be the last of the old-time Swaledale miners, was allowed by the agent to "work t'beck", a relatively soft option to scrambling about underground. And so he did, day after day—excepting Sunday, of course: a solitary figure in the landscape, looking for the glint of lead and, quite sure, he would one day strike it rich.